"I've lived my life without wasting even a minute of it doing things that wouldn't have pleased God."

—Carlo Acutis

Helping You Bring the Joy of the Faith to Your Family

BLESSED CARLO ACUTIS

The Amazing Discovery of a Teenager in Heaven

Sabrina Arena Ferrisi

Foreword by Patrick Novecosky

HOLY HEROES BOOKS
Cramerton, North Carolina

Blessed Carlo Acutis: The Amazing Discovery of a Teenager in Heaven by Sabrina Arena Ferrisi.

Published by Holy Heroes, LLC.
Cramerton, North Carolina
All rights reserved.
HolyHeroes.com

Copyright © 2022 Holy Heroes, LLC. All rights reserved. No portion of this book may be reproduced in any form without permission from the publisher, except as permitted by U.S. copyright law.

Excerpts from the Revised Standard Version of the Bible, 2nd edition, ©1971 by the Division of Christian Education of the National Council of the Churches of Christ in the United States of America. Used by permission. All rights reserved. Some Scripture texts in this work are taken from the New American Bible, revised edition ©2010, 1991, 1986, 1970 Confraternity of Christian Doctrine, Washington, D.C. and are used by permission of the copyright owner. All Rights Reserved. No part of the New American Bible may be reproduced in any form without permission in writing from the copyright owner.

Special thanks to Blessed Carlo's family and friends for photographs including www.MariaVision.it.
Thanks to Lauren Rupar for preliminary design and photo resource assistance and to Edward Jones for additional copy writing.

Cover art and book design by Chris Pelicano.

ISBN: 978-1-936330-98-0

Printed in USA.   First Edition.

HOLY HEROES BOOKS
An Imprint of Holy Heroes, LLC.

"The lives of the saints
are not limited to their earthly biographies
but also include their being and working
in God after death.

In the saints one thing becomes clear:
those who draw near to God
do not withdraw from men,
but rather become truly close to them."

Pope Benedict XVI,
Deus Caritas Est
(God is Love) 40, 42.

DEDICATION

To my husband Leonardo —thank you for your support through these many years of journalism and parenting —and for your greatest gift of always making me laugh.

For my five children —Leo, Francisco, Victoria, Isabella and Nicholas —it has been an honor to parent you and watch you grow with all the unique gifts that God has bestowed on each one of you. Like Carlo —never forget that all of us can be saints in this 21st Century. Making God the center of our lives never leaves us with less. It makes us whole.

—Sabrina Arena Ferrisi

Contents

Foreword	1
How (and Why) the Church Investigates Who is in Heaven	5
Carlo's Life on Earth	13
Carlo's Eucharistic Miracles Website	41
Carlo's Religious Practices and Devotions	47
Carlo's Final Act	61
Congregation of the Causes of Saints: Decree on Virtues	69
Carlo's Life after Death	77
Congregation of the Causes of Saints: The Miracle	80
Relics of Saints	82
Beatification	85
What Comes Next?	87
Official Prayer for the Canonization of Blessed Carlo Acutis	91
Post-Script	93
Carlo's Sayings	96
Carlo's "Kit" for Becoming a Saint	101
Timeline	103
How to Learn More	108
Endnotes	112
About the Author	118

Foreword

In every age since the beginning of time, God has raised up prophets and saints to guide his people and build the Church.

Abraham interceded for Sodom and Gomorrah. Jonah called on Nineveh to repent. Micah and Isaiah predicted the coming of Jesus. Saint Patrick brought the Gospel to Ireland. Saint Joan of Arc saved Catholic France.

In the 1300s, Catherine of Siena called the Pope to leave France and return to Rome. Seven hundred years later, John Paul II preached the New Evangelization and, in the twenty-first century, an Italian teenager is calling us to be all-in for Jesus Christ.

Carlo Acutis is not just your average old saint. (Not your average young saint either!) Although he only lived fifteen years, his passion for the Gospel transformed the lives of thousands during his lifetime—and millions more since his death in 2006.

Saint books can be tough to read. They sometimes get bogged down in obscure details that make you want to quit reading or skip ahead. Not this one.

I've known the author, Sabrina Arena Ferrisi, for a long time. I started editing her work in 2005, and when she told me she was writing a book on Carlo, I was intrigued.

I had heard of Carlo and his passion for the Eucharist. I knew he was Italian and had died young but that's it. Right around the time of his beatification, I read that his relics were on display in Italy and that his body was at least partly incorrupt (without decay).

His family asked that he be dressed in blue jeans and a t-shirt, which happened to be his everyday clothing. His relics were on display for veneration. The news of this remarkable young man made me sit up and take notice.

In these pages, Sabrina has done a remarkable job of capturing Carlo's life through exhaustive research and first-hand interviews with his mother. Reading this book has had a profound impact on me. It made me want to examine my own life. How do I treat the less fortunate? How much time do I spend in prayer? Am I overly attached to my possessions? How focused am I on Jesus?

Carlo Acutis was "all-in" for the Catholic Faith and Our Lord all the time. 24/7. He went out of his way to thank the janitors and doormen at his apartment building and school. He gave his possessions to the homeless and encouraged others to treat them with dignity. I'm not so good at doing things like this, but now that I know his story, I want to do more.

Although Carlo came from a wealthy family, he spent his life detached from money and possession. He found inspiration in the life of Saint Francis of Assisi, who left behind his father's wealth to embrace a life of poverty.

The Amazing Discovery of a Teenager in Heaven

Through his earthly life and example—and through his heavenly intercession—Carlo is destined to become the patron saint of twenty-first-century youth. He proved that with God's grace and a heart fully open to the truth, sanctity is possible for modern teenagers.

Carlo also proved that despite all the challenges young people face in the modern world, the truths of the Faith still resonate and transform the hearts of men and women, girls and boys in every nation across the face of the earth.

Carlo Acutis, pray for us!

Patrick Novecosky

Founder of NovaMedia
Author of *100 Ways John Paul II Changed the World*

How (and Why) the Church Investigates Who is in Heaven

"All Christians are called to be saints. Saints are persons in Heaven (officially canonized or not) ... who are worthy of imitation."
—United States Conference of Catholic Bishops

Every person comes into this world the same way: a uniquely created soul in union with a unique body, created by God.

And every person will leave this world the same way: having that union of soul and body torn apart in death.

However, earthly death is not the end of our lives. You see, God made our souls to be immortal—to live forever—but not in this world.

When God decides to end this world, every person's soul will be reunited with his or her body to live forever in another world which God will create: either resurrected to live in Heaven with God and our loved ones and the angels, or to spend eternity in Hell separated from God, alone with the demons forever.

That's the way God made each one of us.

But the souls we have right now are not capable of living in Heaven. In order to live in Heaven, each person's soul must be transformed into the type of soul that will make us able to be in the very presence of God. God will transform our souls—but He asks us to accept this transformation freely *by cooperating with His grace throughout our lives on Earth.*

The saints are those persons who are in Heaven—so we know they have been transformed through their free cooperation with God to be capable of living in Heaven. We can learn from their lives how we can cooperate with God to be transformed, as well.

How do we know whether someone is a Saint and is already in Heaven?

When the Catholic Church declares someone a Saint, we can know for certain that person is in Heaven.

You see, the Church doesn't "make someone a Saint," but instead the Church carefully reviews a person's life and documents those signs that prove God transformed that person from this life on earth and raised him or her to live with Him in Heaven—right now!

Join us step-by-step through the investigation of Carlo Acutis, a boy who died as a teen in Italy in 2006, as the Church strove to discover whether he is in Heaven today.

Step-by-Step:
The Church's process to discover a Saint in Heaven

1. Popular demand for an investigation

The first step begins after a person's death: those who knew the person petition to have the investigatory process begin. The Church requires that the process normally not begin until at least five years after his or her death. This waiting period is to ensure that the reputation for a person's sanctity is lasting.

When the waiting period has passed, the bishop of the diocese where the person died can ask the Holy See to allow the initialization of a Cause for Beatification and Canonization. The request is reviewed and permission granted to the initiating bishop by communicating *"nihil obstat"* (nothing stands in the way). Once the cause has been accepted by the Vatican, the person is called a Servant of God.

2. The formal Church investigation begins

At this point a thorough investigation is undertaken to determine if the candidate for sainthood lived a life that demonstrated heroic virtue.

The person in charge of moving the investigation forward is called the postulator, and he or she is appointed by the local bishop. The postulator gathers as much information about the candidate as can be found, including all of the candidate's writings, plus testimonies from the people who knew him or her.

This step can take years to complete. Once the investigation is complete, a summary of the findings called a *Positio* is created.

If the diocesan bishop concludes from the *Positio* that the Servant of God did, in fact, live a life of heroic virtue, the *Positio* and all the documentation supporting it are presented to the Congregation for the Causes of Saints at the Vatican for review. If the Congregation approves the cause at this juncture, a Decree of Heroic Virtues is then sent to the pope for his approval.

The pope makes the final determination, judging for the Church whether the Servant of God did indeed live a heroically virtuous life. If he agrees that heroic virtue has been proven, then the Servant of God is henceforth called Venerable.

3. Proof from Heaven is then required

There are now two more stages: Beatification (declared "Blessed") and Canonization (declared a "Saint"). Both stages require proof from Heaven that a person is with God.

For a person to be beatified and recognized as a Blessed, a miracle needs to have occurred *which can be attributed to prayers made to the person after their death*. This miracle provides proof that the candidate for sainthood is already in Heaven and is thus able to intercede with God on others' behalf.

People who have prayed to the Venerable submit to the postulator events they consider miraculous, which could only have occurred through the union of the Venerable with God after death. These miracles are then reviewed and investigated.

Before a miracle is approved by the Congregation for the Causes of Saints, it is subjected to a rigorous review by scientists, doctors, theologians, and other qualified officials. Usually the miracles offered are of medical cures. These medical cures must be instantaneous and lasting.

The investigation is two-fold: first, that the miracle is definitively proven to be unexplainable by natural causes, and second, that the miracle was due to the intercession of the Venerable.

If both criteria are met, a Decree of a Miracle is submitted to the pope.

Again, the pope is required to make the final decision. If he confirms the authenticity of the miracle, a date is set for the beatification ceremony. After this ceremony, veneration of the newly proclaimed Blessed may then be carried on in specified locations.

The Final Step:

4. Canonization

Canonization is the final step in declaring a person a Saint. To reach this stage, a second miracle normally needs to be attributed to prayers made to the candidate *after* they have been beatified. (Martyrs, those killed for the Faith, however, only need one verified miracle to be declared a Saint, because martyrdom itself is recognized as a miracle of grace.) In this way, a sure sign from Heaven is always the final requirement that it is God's Will for a Blessed to be formally recognized as a Saint.

—*The Publisher*

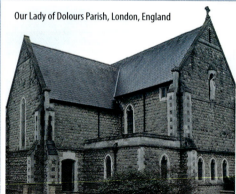

Our Lady of Dolours Parish, London, England

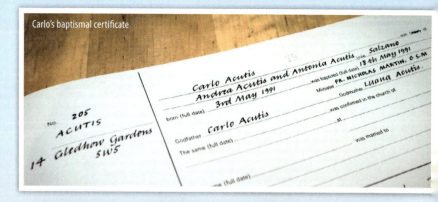

Carlo's baptismal certificate

Carlo in his baptismal gown, held by his grandmother.

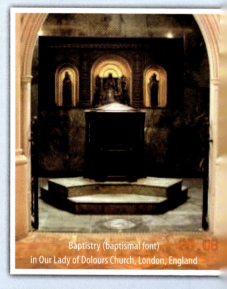

Baptistry (baptismal font) in Our Lady of Dolours Church, London, England

Carlo's Life on Earth

Young Carlo

The birth of every child is a cause for joy. This was certainly the case for one English-born Italian boy named Carlo Acutis.

Carlo was born in London on May 3, 1991, and his Italian parents were filled with incredible happiness because he was their first-born son. Good-paying jobs had brought Carlo's dad, Andrea, and mom, Antonia, to England. Little did they know that their son Carlo would be a cause for celebration and amazement—not just for themselves and their family—but eventually for young people and adults around the world.

Carlo was baptized in the parish of Our Lady of Dolours in London. His maternal and paternal grandparents were there, as well as his aunt and great-grandmother, all of whom had flown in from Italy for the special occasion.[1]

From the beginning, Carlo was an extremely happy, observant baby who was known for his wide smile. He spoke his first word,

Carlo and his mother, Antonia.

"papa," at three months, and his second word, "mama," at four months.[2]

Because both Andrea and Antonia worked full time, they needed to hire a nanny immediately for baby Carlo.

The first nannies were English women who did their job extremely well, though sometimes—as inevitably happens—there were bumps in the road.[3]

There was the day when the Acutis parents found a Scottish nanny asleep with baby Carlo in her arms. The two had dark stains on their shirts that looked frighteningly like dried blood. His horrified parents quickly woke up baby Carlo and his nanny, only to learn that she had been eating chocolate before the nap, and the chocolate had melted on their shirts![4]

Another nanny had started dipping Carlo's pacifier in a British syrup from the pharmacy to calm him down when he cried. The pacifier worked all too well until his parents discovered that the syrup contained alcohol. The syrup was promptly thrown away.[5]

When Carlo was four months old, his family moved back to Milan, Italy, where they lived for the rest of his life. His parents hired a Polish nanny named Beata. She proved to be very important in Carlo's life. The nanny had a great love for Pope Saint John Paul II, the great Polish pope who led the Roman Catholic Church from 1978 to 2005.[6]

Beata would sometimes mention God to Carlo when he was a toddler, but around the time the boy was four years old, he began to act and speak in ways that surprised his parents. Carlo began to ask them about God, about Jesus and Mary.

Young Carlo with his nanny, Beata.

When he went for walks with his parents around Milan, he would ask them if he could go inside every Church they passed. Carlo wanted to say hello to Jesus and would often kiss the feet of statues depicting Our Lord. Other times, he wanted to bring flowers and leave them in front of statues of Mary.

Carlo's tremendous religious fervor shocked his parents because they had never talked about religion with him at all!

In fact, Andrea and Antonia were not practicing Catholics, though Andrea had always considered himself to be religious. He went to Sunday Mass from time to time but not every week. Antonia never went at all.[7]

"By the time, I had gotten married, I had been to Church a total of three times—my baptism, communion, and confirmation," said Antonia.[8]

When Carlo began to ask questions about the Catholic Faith, Antonia was at a loss. Though she was an educated, successful businesswoman, she could not answer Carlo's simple questions.

An Awakening of Faith

After struggling with Carlo's questions, Antonia decided to talk to a friend who was a devout Catholic. The friend suggested that Antonia meet with a priest whom she knew—Father Ilio Carrai—who was known as the "Padre Pio" of Bologna, Italy. When Antonia went to meet Father Carrai, he told her to take a theology class.[9]

Despite her busy schedule as a working mom, Antonia enrolled in a theology class in Milan. The main reason for doing so was because she wanted to answer Carlo's questions properly. She wanted to be able to answer his difficult questions.

That theology class changed her life. Through it, Antonia rediscovered the beauty of her Catholic faith, and in the years that followed, whenever Carlo would ask questions about God, she would be right there next to him looking for the answers because now *she* was interested, too.

While Antonia began her spiritual journey of learning the Catholic faith as an adult, little Carlo turned four. His parents decided to send him to a public kindergarten school in Milan called Parco Pagani. Carlo was ecstatic because he loved to be around other children.

During these early years, Carlo's natural goodness and love for God shocked his family because they saw him developing true holiness that was independent of his family and school.

"The presence of God was inside of him," his mother said. "It was very personal. His generosity and purity were something he had his whole life until death. He had a sense of the dignity of life. From the time he was four or five years old, he was very generous, obedient, and docile. And he was devoted to Jesus."[11]

Carlo continued to ask questions about God all the time. In doing so, he pulled his parents into a life of deeper faith and supernatural awareness.

Antonia would end up studying theology for twelve years. Father Carrai became her spiritual director. And when Carlo was older, Father Carrai became his spiritual director as well.[12]

An Ordinary Childhood

When Carlo was ready to enter the first grade, his parents enrolled him in the Saint Carlo Institute of Milan. However, after three months, they decided to transfer him to the Tommaseo Institute run by the Sisters of Saint Marcellina because this school was closer to their home. Carlo stayed in this school, completing his elementary and middle school years there.[13]

The nuns who worked in this school say that Carlo was always smiling and surrounded by friends. He never failed to greet the nuns who worked at the front door every day.[14]

Carlo befriended another group of people at the school: the custodians who cleaned the school. Most of these men were foreigners who had come to work in Italy. As a matter of fact, Carlo was the only child who greeted them. Most of the janitors were Muslim or Hindu, but Carlo did not care if they were poor or of a different religion or race. He would always greet them in the morning and the afternoon, often stopping to chat with them.[15]

Even the doormen in the apartment building where he grew up say that Carlo always stopped to speak to them. Carlo was humble, even though he came from a wealthy family. He treated everybody with respect.[16]

Like so many children, Carlo watched cartoons. His favorite cartoon TV show was *Pokémon*, and his favorite cartoon character was Pikachu. Carlo was also very good at drawing these characters and he kept notebooks of his sketches.[17]

During middle school, Carlo would often meet his friends after

"Carlo saved me. He was the one who got me to start my spiritual journey. In my youth, there was a superficiality to my faith. But it was Carlo who pushed me to do research, and I began to reflect on life. Carlo pushed me to read."[10] —Antonia Acutis

Young Carlo loved his pets.

school and go to a local sports center or play outside in the town square, called a piazza. Sometimes they would go to Carlo's house after school and watch cartoons.

As he got older, Carlo liked to watch television. He enjoyed police shows and quiz shows that tested contestants about general culture.[18]

Carlo loved riding his bicycle around the neighborhood. He also enjoyed karate, soccer, basketball, skiing, and canoeing. In addition, Carlo loved music and taught himself how to play the saxophone. When it came to toys, he never wanted to have many. Antonia said that most families she knew had far more toys for their children than Carlo.

Summers were special for Carlo. From May to September, he spent time with his maternal grandparents in a small town named Centola in the south of Italy. His great-grandparents had met in this town. Carlo's great-grandmother had been born in New York City, not far from where the Twin Towers (now Ground Zero) once stood, only to return to Centola when she was fifteen years old. She was known to be a saintly woman who helped many poor people in the area—so much so that people in the town still pray for her intercession.[19]

On those summer days, Carlo liked going to the beach and picking fruit off his grandparents' trees. The townspeople say he was known as a friendly boy who always said hello to everyone.[20]

Carlo also loved to visit his father's parents in Turin, Italy. Sometimes, when his family went to visit these grandparents, Carlo spent time in the kitchen watching the family's cook prepare the meal. At one point, Carlo decided that he wanted to be a great

Carlo and his soccer teammates.

Carlo having fun.

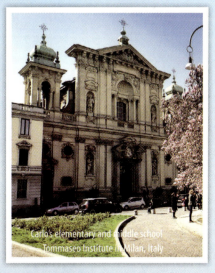
Carlo's elementary and middle school Tommaseo Institute in Milan, Italy

Some of Carlo's hobbies included riding his bicycle, karate, soccer, basketball, skiing, and canoeing.

chef, just like the grandparents' chef. This cook would later recall that Carlo was unique in his quest for knowledge—and also for his good manners. The chef had worked for many wealthy people before the Acutis family, but he had never seen a boy Carlo's age make a point of thanking him for the meal every single day.[21]

Carlo loved to spend time talking with his paternal grandfather, listening to his advice, and playing chess with him.

The child also loved his two grandmothers. One was half Irish and half Polish, the other a full-blooded Italian. Both women had come from deeply Catholic families—and both said that they had never seen a child as holy as Carlo.

When Carlo was four years old, his maternal grandfather died. Shortly after his death, he appeared to Carlo[22] asking for prayers to get him out of Purgatory. Carlo insisted that it was not a dream, but that his grandfather had actually appeared to him from Purgatory to ask for prayers.

This experience made a big impact on Carlo. He knew that by interceding for loved ones who have died, one can help them get out of Purgatory and into Heaven. He also knew that by making small sacrifices and offering them up for the sake of those persons in Purgatory, one could help them reach Heaven more quickly.

"He was always making sacrifices for sinners," Carlo's mother said. "He would say 'No' to desserts, 'No' to video games or films, and offer that up for sinners. He meditated on Hell. He would say, 'Do you realize what it would be like to be in Hell forever?' He knew that the greatest battle was within us."[23]

Not long after Carlo's grandfather died, his maternal grandmother, Luana, now a widow, moved to Milan to be closer to her only daughter, Antonia, and her family.[24]

It's a Dog and Cat's Life

Everyone who spent time with Carlo knew about his love for animals. His all-time favorite activity throughout his childhood was playing with his dogs.

The Acutis family had four dogs, two cats, and a red goldfish. The cats were Bambi and Cleopatra. The dogs were named Briciola (Crumb), Stellina (Little Star), Poldo, and Chiara (Claire). Carlo's favorite dog, Briciola, was a Miniature Pinscher.[25]

Briciola would steal Carlo's favorite stuffed toy—Pikachu—every day and hide it somewhere in the house. Carlo would find it and hide it in his closet. However, Briciola would somehow find his way back to Carlo's closet and bark until it was given to him. This ongoing war over Pikachu went on every day for years.[26]

One summer, the Acutis family decided to go on a road trip to Spain. Carlo brought Briciola, who was only three months old at the time. The Acutis family also brought Carlo's grandmother, Luana, on the vacation. She often carried Briciola in her purse wherever they went.

One day they decided to visit a monastery of Poor Clare nuns, which was right next to a beautiful museum where dogs were not allowed. Luana could not bear the thought of leaving little Briciola alone in the hotel, so she decided to hide the dog in her purse. She brought him with her on a guided tour. During the tour (which took a long time), the guide would stop the group every now and then and ask everyone to stand in silence and meditate in front of a work of art.

During these moments of silence, Briciola would suddenly bark from within the grandmother's purse. Luana was mortified. To cover for him, she would cough every time the dog barked.

The tour guide stopped and said, "What was that? Where did that come from?" Carlo's grandmother coughed. The dog barked again. She coughed again. It was all that Carlo and his parents could do not to explode in laughter over the situation. Ultimately, the tour guide never figured out where the mysterious barking was coming from—and Carlo filmed the entire event with his video camera.[27]

Making movies with his camera became Carlo's passion in middle school. It was only natural that he began to make movies about his dogs, thus uniting his two passions—moviemaking and playing with his pets—into one activity.

Carlo often made films with his cousin, Flavia, and the dogs. They became the stars of these little films. He called his film series "Stellina, the Chubby One" after his dog Stellina, who was decidedly overweight. Carlo nicknamed Briciola "the dog with the seven demons" because it had a very angry side when provoked. Chiara, the "supreme rat" in the films, was the terror of all the other dogs in the Acutis household. She would growl at anyone who encroached upon her territory, which consisted of Antonia Acutis' side of the room.[28]

Carlo and his cousins wrote a script where the dogs were pitted against the cats, over whom they would become the masters of the universe (or of the Acutis apartment). Each dog had its own lines with voice-overs done by Carlo. He would spend hours making these movies with his cousins. Friends and family thought the videos were so good that perhaps Carlo would become a film director when he grew up.[29]

Carlo's love for animals went beyond his pets. Whenever he found a hurt or abandoned animal in the street, he would bring it home. He hoped that animals would go to Heaven, even though this is not an official teaching of the Church. When Carlo read a story about Pope Saint Paul VI, who once told a child who had lost his dog that he would surely see the pet again—he was comforted to conclude that at least this Pope believed that "all dogs go to Heaven."[30]

Carlo also loved dolphins. Once, when Carlo was twelve years old, he went out on a boat ride with his mother and grandparents. Carlo told his mother before the trip that he had asked Jesus to let him see dolphins out at sea. Dolphins are not normally seen in this area, so they told Carlo not to get his hopes up.

They had gone out far from the Italian coastal town of Santa Margherita Ligure when suddenly their boat was surrounded by dozens of dolphins! This incredible and unique spectacle lasted about half an hour, amazing and delighting everyone on board.[31]

Falling in Love with the Eucharist

Carlo developed a deep devotion to the Eucharist as a young child. As soon as he learned that the unleavened bread offered at Holy Mass—after the prayers of Consecration—becomes the Body and Blood of Jesus, he wanted to be allowed to receive Holy Communion right away. At the age of six, he asked his parents if he could get special permission to receive the Eucharist earlier than the Italian norm, which is nine years of age.

After some discussion with his pastor, Father Aldo Locatelli, Carlo was permitted to receive his First Holy Communion at the age of seven. His family decided that Carlo's special day would be June 16—about six weeks after his seventh birthday—at the Convent of the Romite Sisters of Saint Ambrose in Perego.[32]

On the way to his first Communion, the family passed a shepherd crossing the road with a little lamb on his shoulders. Carlo was thrilled because he loved lambs, but also because he felt it was a sign from God.

After receiving his first Communion, Carlo went to Mass every day from the age of seven until he died at the age of fifteen. On that rare occasion when he could not go to Mass, he would say a prayer of spiritual communion.

Years later, when Carlo was a young teenager, his pastor, Monsignor Gianfranco Poma of Santa Maria Segreta Church in Milan, recalled the first time he saw Carlo sitting in front of the tabernacle, quietly praying. He asked Carlo if he came often to pray there.

Carlo replied that he did come often because it taught him how to be a "light" in different aspects of his life—at home with his parents and at school with his peers. Eucharistic adoration helped Carlo learn to be a guide for others, helping them to see Jesus working in their lives.[33]

Young Carlo was very sensitive to the way priests celebrated

Santa Maria Segreta, Carlo's parish church in Milan, Italy

Carlo on the day of his First Holy Communion, June 16, 1998.

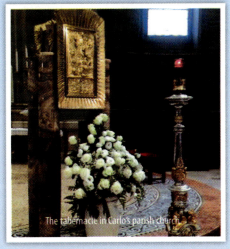

The tabernacle in Carlo's parish church

Because Carlo was so fascinated with the Person of Jesus, he recognized that receiving Him in the Eucharist was a real encounter. He believed that the Eucharist fed his soul and made it possible for him to be like Christ and give of himself to others.

the Mass. He could sense when a priest was truly reverent. Conversely, Carlo would become sad when he noticed priests who did not put their hearts into celebrating Mass.

In 2005, during World Youth Day in Cologne, Germany, Pope Benedict XVI celebrated Mass in front of one million young people in a field called Marienfeld. Carlo watched the entire Mass on television from his home in Italy.

He was greatly impressed when the pope lifted the Eucharist high and said, "God must be adored on your knees and in silence." Everyone in the field got down on their knees in the wet ground, and a great silence came over the immense crowd.

Pope Benedict then spoke to the priests: "Let yourselves be drawn always anew by the Holy Eucharist, in the communion of life with Christ. Consider it as the center of every day the capacity to celebrate in a worthy manner. Lead men over and over again to this Mystery."[34]

Friends with the Saints

When Carlo learned how to read, he read the usual Italian children's books. But he also began to read about Saints and the Bible. One Saint who captured his imagination was Saint Francis of Assisi.

Carlo and his family began to visit Assisi as pilgrims when he was very young. They liked it so much that they kept returning and, eventually, they decided to buy a house there. Carlo would stay there for long periods and most holidays. Many people in this small city still remember him.

The Amazing Discovery of a Teenager in Heaven

Carlo believed that Saint Francis of Assisi was one of his protectors—perhaps because they shared a few things in common. Both Carlo and Francis were born into wealthy families and desired to live simply. Both held a passionate belief in the Real Presence of Jesus in the Eucharist. And both had a desire to help the poorest of the poor.

Carlo enjoyed visits to his relatives throughout Italy. But Assisi was one of Carlo's favorite places, because he was so devoted to Saint Francis of Assisi.

During his vacations in Assisi, Carlo would often see his cousins. They would go to Mass every day and then walk to Monte Subasio, which is about six miles from Assisi. Here the hills were steep, and the cousins would play with their dogs, fly kites, or pretend to be explorers with treasure maps. Then they would go to a local swimming pool.[35]

When Carlo was in high school and he would tell his schoolmates that he was going to Assisi for vacation, some would make fun of him. They would tell him that he could afford to go to more exotic places—like Hawaii. Why go to Assisi?[36] Carlo shrugged off their taunts. He told his spiritual director that Assisi was the place where he felt the happiest. He was so drawn to Assisi that, before his death, he told his parents he wanted to be buried there.

Carlo also had a devotion to Saints Dominic Savio, Bernadette, Padre Pio, Gemma Galgani, the three shepherd children of Fatima—Lucia, Jacinta, and Francisco—Anthony of Padua, and Tarcisius, who was martyred for the Eucharist. He also had a deep devotion to Our Lady of Pompeii.[37]

These Saints were not just people he had read about. They were people whom he tried to learn from. He was especially interested in the lives of young Saints like Saint Bernadette, who was only fourteen years old when she experienced eighteen apparitions of the Virgin Mary between February 11 and July 16, 1858.

It amazed him that Bernadette was illiterate and could not even speak French, but only a regional dialect. It seemed to Carlo that Bernadette was chosen to receive these great apparitions precisely because of her great humility and lack of education.

Carlo considered these Saints as friends in Heaven to whom he could pray for help.

It Gets So Cold in the Winter

Milan is full of homeless people who live on the streets, even in the winter when temperatures drop below freezing.

Carlo was so upset about people living in the streets of Milan that he began to go outside at night at the age of nine to bring food and drink to the homeless. He always went with an adult—either with Rajesh or another household helper named Sheyla. Sometimes Carlo's mom would go, too. Carlo would, at times, use his own money to buy blankets and sleeping bags for the men and women he encountered. Incredibly, Carlo went out most evenings—especially during the wintertime.

He did concrete things to help the poor. There was a beggar named Emmanuele who slept on the steps of a church in a cardboard box. Carlo used his savings to buy him a sleeping bag. He would save a little of his dinner and bring it to the man, night after night. Then one day, without warning, Carlo went to find Emmanuele and could not find him. They never saw him again, which broke Carlo's heart.

Another time, Carlo and his mother found a homeless woman named Giuseppina who was bleeding. She would not eat or drink anything. They realized that she was in danger of dying and called an ambulance. She ended up being hospitalized for forty days. Their action saved her life.[38]

Carlo brought thermos flasks, sleeping bags, and warm food to the homeless with the support of his parents. He also donated his pocket money to the Capuchin aid organization, Opera San Francesco, in Milan, which gives food for the poor.[39]

Sometimes his mother had to force Carlo to buy clothes for himself because he didn't want to. "He said that what he had was enough and that the rest should go to the poor," she said.[40]

During his holidays in Assisi, Carlo helped the homeless there, too. When he went to walk his dogs, he discovered that a homeless man was sleeping in the public gardens at night. He asked his grandmother, Luana, to prepare some food to bring the man. He would also leave one euro of his allowance next to the sleeping man so he would find it in the morning.[41]

The Battle is Within

Carlo became an assistant Catechism teacher at the age of eleven. Those who knew him were impressed that he read the Bible every day, as well as the *Catechism of the Catholic Church*. Carlo was capable of memorizing everything he read.

By thirteen, he was teaching his own catechism class. Carlo read many Italian Catholic magazines and newspapers to keep up with the Catholic faith and current events. He was always able to explain Christianity in a way that was relevant to children and his peers.

At Carlo's high school, whenever religion teachers could not remember a Bible verse or found it difficult to explain a concept in a way that students could understand, they would ask Carlo.

His fellow students recall that Carlo was often better at explaining religious concepts than the teachers.[42]

Carlo noticed that many of his peers had a problem with certain religious concepts because their parents never took them to Mass. He would explain this information with younger children in a way that they could understand.

Antonia noted that while most people his age lived "horizontally"—only looking at life on Earth—Carlo lived his life vertically, referring everything to God and eternal life in Heaven.[43]

At a certain point in Carlo's life, he began to ask himself the difficult questions: Who am I? Where do I come from? Why am I here? He answered all of these questions in the context of Jesus Christ as his best friend. Carlo always lived in God's presence and was in a constant relationship with God.[44]

Carlo knew his shortcomings. He had to work on talking too much, eating too much, and not concentrating when praying. He was aware of his weaknesses and made an effort to work on them. He went to Confession regularly, and his mother noted that he kept a journal in which he reflected on his behavior and how he could improve himself.[45]

His paternal grandfather encouraged Carlo to be temperate with food. Eventually, Carlo was able to grow in this virtue.[46] Carlo once wrote in his notebook, "What does it matter if you can win one thousand battles, but cannot win against your own corrupt passions?"[47]

A Friend in Need

Carlo often helped his friends with homework. Although Carlo was never the top student in his class, he did well academically. His best subject was math.[48]

In middle school, one of his friends needed to present his thesis and was worried about the presentation. Despite his workload, Carlo prepared a PowerPoint presentation for his friend to help him out.[49]

A girl in Carlo's eighth-grade class had serious problems at school in passing her exams. Carlo decided to tutor her for free, and he helped her pass all her exams.[50]

Carlo also looked out for kids who were bullied. One student in his elementary school was mentally handicapped and was often bullied by classmates. Carlo defended him every time.[51]

Carlo was well-liked because of his open personality, generosity, humility, and positive outlook. When kids were being left out, Carlo would take them by the arm and invite them back into the group.

He was very attentive to the sufferings of other children who were going through family problems. If a classmate had parents who were getting divorced, Carlo made a special effort to invite them to his home. In fact, the kids going through hard times within their own families were the ones he most often invited over.[52]

Carlo also had a great deal of patience with little children, sometimes playing with the younger kids during school lunchtime. His relatives often noted how Carlo would patiently play with young cousins when they visited.

"Carlo was like every other kid except that he had this immense faith. It was like a thing that burst out of him. His childlike self and his faith walked together—one did not hide from the other," said his cousin, Flavia.[53]

Rajesh Mohur—a servant who worked in the Acutis household—noted that Carlo was much more mature than the average child his age. Despite the family's wealth, Carlo was, amazingly, not spoiled.

"What struck me about Carlo was his deep faith and generosity. I never met a child who went to Mass every day and who recited the Rosary every day and who did Eucharistic adoration," he said.[54]

Another thing that shocked Rajesh was that Carlo decided at one point to set his alarm clock fifteen minutes earlier than usual every day so that he could get up and make his bed—thus sparing Rajesh the work of making it.[55]

Carlo and the man he called "my trusty friend Rajesh."

Rajesh eventually converted to Catholicism because of his friendship with Carlo. Several of his Indian friends living in Milan, who got to know Carlo, also converted to the Faith.

Carlo knew that examples were very important in the Christian life, but he also knew that words were important, too. He often spoke about the Catholic Faith to friends, how the goal in life has to be "the infinite." Sometimes, when he was helping friends with computer problems, he would talk about eternal life.

The World of Computer Science

Carlo's intense interest in computer programming began when he was only eight years old. At first, he began to read computer magazines. Then he asked his mother to buy him books.

Antonia looked for computer programming books for children but could not find any. Instead, she bought him college-level textbooks. "He would use these books alone and he could do everything with Photoshop, Maya, and 3D animation. He was incredible," said Antonia.[56]

Once he mastered programming, Carlo began using his skills to spread the Catholic faith.

During his first year in high school, Carlo worked with a university student to create the website for his parish, Santa Maria Segreta in Milan. The student felt encouraged to do his computer science studies well—all because of Carlo's enthusiasm. Another time, a famous Italian computer programmer came to the Acutis family's home because of his friendship with Carlo's father. Upon meeting Carlo and talking about programming, he was left speechless because Carlo knew almost as much as he did.[57]

Carlo created another website for his high school to promote community service. "All of this he did with a simple laptop," Antonia explained. "Carlo believed that the Internet could be an 'atomic bomb' for good—but it could also be used for bad things which diminish the human person."[58]

Carlo worried about how the virtual world could take people away from the real world, such that a person could lose their sense of reality. Or how a person could get depressed because something they posted on social media did not get enough "likes."[59]

He found it strange that people would put their own pictures on the Internet. For him, God had to be in the first place, not the self. For example, when he was 14 years old and his exhibit on Eucharistic Miracles went to the Vatican in 2005, Carlo did not allow his name to be on the exhibit—not because he wasn't proud of it, but, rather, he did not want to draw attention to himself. The attention had to be on God.[60]

After Carlo's death, Pope Francis wrote three full paragraphs about Carlo in a document called *Christus Vivit* (2019). The pope said that Carlo had always used the Internet for good.

"Carlo was well-aware that the whole apparatus of communications, advertising and social networking can be used to lull us, to make us addicted to consumerism and buying the latest thing on the market, obsessed with our free time, caught up in negativity.

Yet he knew how to use the new communications technology to transmit the Gospel, to communicate values and beauty." (*Christus Vivit*, 105)

Carlo had full confidence in the potential of mass media—if it was used well—to evangelize the world. He thought that technology should be used in every way possible to spread the Faith because it could reach the most people.

Countless of Carlo's friends remembered how he would help them with their computers and would teach them how to prepare school presentations. One mother remembered that when her daughter had forgotten her password, Carlo came to their home and restored it. "He saved me from having to buy a new computer for my daughter," she recalled.[61]

His classmates realized that Carlo was not only a computer genius but that, by his example, he had taught them the right way to use computers, which otherwise can become a source of addiction and sin.

Eucharistic Miracles

When Carlo was growing up in Milan, he would often see people standing for hours in long lines to get tickets for rock concerts. As his mother, Antonia would say: "…with people literally ripping their hair out to get these tickets."[62]

There were no lineups, however, in front of Milan's hundreds of churches. Inside, the churches were virtually abandoned.

"Why are the churches empty?" Carlo would ask his mother.

"Don't people realize that Jesus is with us? There should be long lines for that."[63]

The whole idea of churches being empty bothered Carlo. In 2005, when Pope Saint John Paul II died, two million people stood in line to walk past his coffin in Rome. Why couldn't people do the same for Jesus, he wondered, hidden in every church's tabernacle?[64]

Antonia remembers Carlo saying,

"The Earth is the same geologically as it has been for thousands of years, but for two thousand years now, we have had the physical presence of Jesus on Earth. It has been super-naturalized. God is living among us. This should give us peace."[65]

At the age of eleven, Carlo began to assist in teaching Catechism to children in his parish. He realized very quickly that most children (and their parents) did not truly understand the Eucharist well at all.

To inspire more excitement about the Eucharist, Carlo began to investigate Eucharistic miracles, starting with what happened in Lanciano, Italy, in the eighth century. A priest had a crisis of faith and stopped believing in the Real Presence of Jesus in the Eucharist.

Nevertheless, the priest continued to celebrate daily Mass. After saying the prayers of Consecration one day, the priest witnessed the Eucharist become a piece of flesh in his hands and the chalice of wine turn to blood. This amazing miracle reignited the monk's faith.[66] The miraculous flesh is still with us today and exhibited in the Church of San Francesco in Lanciano, Italy.

Centuries later, the host was examined by several groups of scientists. The flesh is identified as human heart tissue. The blood is type AB, the same as that found on the Shroud of Turin and in every other Eucharistic Miracle which has been investigated.

The protein content of the blood in Lanciano is in the same proportion as fresh blood, and there is no evidence of any chemicals used to preserve it. The fact that the flesh and blood have not decomposed in twelve centuries cannot be explained by science.[67]

Carlo decided to research all Eucharistic miracles around the world throughout the centuries and create a website to catalog all of them. He worked on this project for four years.[68]

Today, the website has been translated into seventeen languages. It also generated an exhibit that traveled in Italy for a few months before Carlo died. After his death, the exhibit traveled to ten thousand parishes on five continents.[69]

Carlo hoped that once people learned about Eucharistic miracles, they would go back to receiving the Eucharist—and see it as a fountain of grace.

He also created exhibits on angels and demons, Hell and Purgatory, and approved Marian apparitions.[70] These exhibits were a way for Carlo to teach others about the Catholic faith.

High School Years

Carlo attended a private Jesuit high school in Milan called Leo XIII Institute. Almost immediately, Carlo threw himself into several

Carlo's Eucharistic Miracles Website
www.miracolieucaristici.org/en/liste/list.html

Carlo's website features 163 true stories of Eucharistic miracles. Where possible, Carlo traveled with his parents to the places in Europe where these miracles had taken place. For locations outside of Europe, Carlo asked people living in those cities or towns to send him photographs to put on his website.

In addition to his website about Eucharistic miracles, Carlo created websites on Angels and Demons, Hell and Purgatory, and Marian Apparitions.

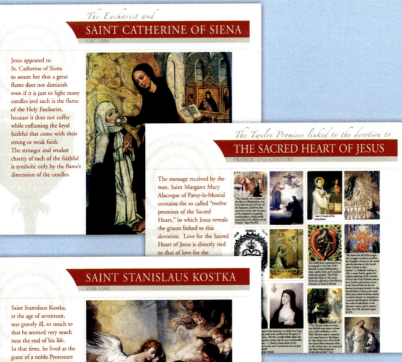

These are some screen shots taken from pages on Carlo's Eucharistic Miracles website.

Eucharistic Miracle of
LANCIANO
ITALY, 750 A.D.

The Flesh and the Blood of Lanciano therefore are just the same as they would be if they had been drawn that very day from a living being.

The reliquary from the 18th century containing the Host and the coagulated Blood, gift of the generous citizen Domenico Colli

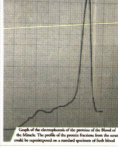

Graph of the electrophoresis of the proteins of the Blood of the Miracle. The profile of the protein fractions from the serum could be superimposed on a standard specimen of fresh blood.

The 5 clots of Blood as seen with a magnifying glass. In the blood of the Miracle can be recognized all the components present in fresh blood, and the miracle within the miracle, each of the 5 clots of Blood weighs 15.85 grams, which is the identical weight of the 5 clots weighed together !

The muscular fiber cells

Histological view of the Flesh

The Church of St. Francis was constructed almost 500 years later, in 1258, above the chapel where the miracle took place

The flesh consists of part of the myocardium, more precisely of the left ventricle. The arteries and veins can be easily identified, as well as a double, slender branch of the vagus nerve. At the time of the miracle, the flesh was living and thus submitted to the law of rigor mortis.

The miracle was the object of several official acknowledgements on the part of the ecclesiastical authorities between 1574 and 1886, not to mention most recently, in 1970, when it was subjected to a scientific examination carried out by professors from the University of Siena, which concluded: "The flesh is true human flesh (formed by muscular tissue from the heart); that the blood is true blood (belonging to the same blood type AB as the flesh); that the component substances are those of human tissues, normal and fresh; that the conservation of the flesh and the blood, left in their natural state for twelve centuries and exposed to the influence of atmospheric and biological elements, remains an extraordinary phenomenon." (The Linoli Report 4/31/1971).

A vagus nerve

Analysis of the Host. Endocardic structures

A small lobe of adipose tissue

Cubical lattice in gold-plated cast iron in which the relics were preserved for almost 266 years, today returned to the Valsecca family chapel

An antique painting depicting the Miracle

This page from Carlo's Eucharistic Miracles website documents the famous Miracle of Lanciano.

activities. Besides his computer programming activities, Carlo also volunteered to help teach catechism to a local confirmation class, an activity he truly enjoyed. The students in his class were fascinated with Carlo's teaching style.

That same year, Carlo began to work on a video for his high school to encourage students to volunteer for community service. The theme he developed for the video was "Volunteering is You." He spent most of the summer of 2006 working on the project. Because Carlo was so gifted in videography, as well as computer programming, he became a natural leader on the project.[71]

Just as he had in elementary school and middle school, Carlo became friends with many students, teachers, and custodians. On the days he entered the school by a side door, he would make a detour at lunchtime just to say hello to the school's doorman because he had missed him in the morning.[72]

Carlo found it easy to make friends in high school. Yet, he always looked out for boys and girls who were somehow isolated and alone, talking to them and encouraging them. Classmates recognized his ability to be friendly and generous, as well as his capacity to be self-disciplined. He was genuinely interested in others.[73] Years later, when his schoolmates remembered Carlo, one of them said,

"If you were in a bad mood, spending time with him would make your bad mood go away."[74]

Whenever discussions among the students on matters of faith and morals came up, Carlo would present the Catholic position without ever disrespecting students who may have had another opinion. He was deeply pro-life and defended the right to life of unborn children and the terminally ill. He also defended Catholic teaching on marriage and family.[75]

Carlo also had very clear ideas on dating. He strongly opposed a boy using a girl's affection for selfish purposes. He also got upset with girls giving themselves physically to the boys they were dating. On more than one occasion he scolded female friends on this subject.[76]

He was known for being smart, but never overbearing. No one was ever jealous of Carlo because he was positive and funny, always trying to help others. Friends say he never bragged about anything, and he wouldn't speak badly about others behind their backs. One of his classmates recalls Carlo's kindness in October of their first year in high school together.

"One day, when we got out of school, we were getting our bicycles to go home, and I confided in him that I was afraid that when the first grades would come out, I would see a return of the teasing and insults that characterized my elementary and middle school years. (In Italy, grades are displayed for all to see on classroom walls.) Carlo calmed me down and told me that if I ever needed help, he would always be available to help me."[77]

Carlo was known in the school for being passionate about his Catholic faith. In high school, he continued going to daily Mass and praying the Rosary every day. Many of his closest friends were not practicing the Faith, but they still loved spending time with Carlo because he was such a good friend.

Although Carlo was the only child in a wealthy Italian family, he never spoke about money or bragged about anything.

Fashion was among the least of Carlo's interests. He tended to wear simple, classic clothes rather than designer apparel, even though his family could afford it. Milan has a long-established history in the fields of fashion, textiles, and clothing design. For Carlo to simply refuse to go along with fashion trends was bold. He was uncomfortable owning more clothes or shoes than necessary.[78]

Carlo was always conscious about not wasting time. A clear example was his approach to video games. He had a *PlayStation*®, and he liked to play video games. But he decided *on his own* to limit his playing time to one hour per week. When his mother asked him why, he told her that he did not want to waste time.

During the process of Carlo's beatification, the Vatican cataloged Carlo's entire Internet search history and discovered that every query had been for evangelization purposes. He had not wasted his time on idle internet searches.

When people would ask him what he wanted to be when he grew up, he would say, "Who knows? But being close to Jesus is my life's plan."

Carlo on the day of his First Holy Communion.

Carlo's Religious Practices and Devotions

Not only was Carlo a pious child, but he was incredibly knowledgeable about many devotions in the Catholic Church. He was a voracious reader and instructed everyone he encountered about the truths of the Faith. Here are a few of the devotions close to his heart.

The Blessed Virgin Mary

Carlo prayed the Rosary every day and consecrated himself to the Virgin Mary many times. He believed that without Mary's help, the path to imitating Jesus was more difficult.[79]

The teen was deeply devoted to Fatima. He loved the story of the three shepherd children in Portugal who were visited by the Blessed Virgin Mary several times in 1917. Carlo was able to visit Fatima a few months before he died. Visiting this place was an incredibly emotional experience for him—especially the Chapel of the Apparitions, as well as the homes of Lucia, Jacinta, and Francisco. Carlo often reflected on their story.[80]

He worried a great deal about people who were lost to Hell, which is one of the main messages of Fatima. He prayed a great deal for sinners, and he tried to make the truths about Hell and Purgatory more known to people through exhibits so that they could avoid sin and its consequences. He always had in mind the danger of each person losing his or her soul.

During a car trip with his parents one summer, Carlo spent most of the time reading a book out loud on Fatima written by Sister Lucia, one of the Fatima visionaries. At one point, he read how Francisco had asked the Blessed Mother if he would go to Heaven. She responded that he would have to pray many more rosaries in order to get to Heaven. When Carlo read this, he was shocked. He told his parents, "If Francisco, who was a small child, was not ready to go to Heaven, what about me, a sinner?"[81]

Carlo was able to meet a nun in Fatima whose grandfather had witnessed the great miracle of the sun, which occurred on October 13, 1917. The nun explained that when the sun danced and appeared to plunge toward Earth, that miracle had been visible in many other cities in Portugal, thus proving that what people in Fatima had witnessed could not have been a collective hallucination.[82]

Besides the story of Fatima, Carlo was also devoted to Lourdes. A spring of water welled up on the spot where the Blessed Mother instructed Saint Bernadette to dig. This famous spring would become the site of countless healing miracles that continue today. Carlo visited Lourdes shortly before he turned twelve.

Carlo's exhibit on all the major apparitions of Our Lady was another way to teach people about these messages from Heaven.

"How is it possible that people are ignoring the appeals of Our Lady?" he would ask.[83]

For Carlo, Mary was a second mother. He prayed to her constantly.

The Sacred Heart of Jesus

Carlo knew the story of Jesus' apparitions to Saint Mary Margaret Alacoque well, especially the promises Jesus made to all who venerate His Sacred Heart by going to Mass and Confession every first Friday of the month.

Over the centuries, there had emerged in Christianity an overemphasis on God as a harsh judge Who is distant from human affairs. When Jesus appeared to Mary Margaret between 1673 and 1675, He revealed that His heart burned with love for humanity and only wanted love and devotion in return. The message of Jesus' Sacred Heart emphasized God's infinite mercy.

Carlo convinced his entire

Carlo was devoted to the practice of the Five First Saturdays of the month, which was revealed to Sister Lucia of Fatima by the Blessed Virgin in 1925: Whoever receives Communion on the first Saturdays of the month, plus Confession and the recitation of the Rosary, and spends fifteen minutes meditating on the Mysteries of the Rosary, intending to offer reparation to offenses against Mary's Immaculate Heart—is promised Mary's assistance at the hour of death with all the graces necessary for their salvation.

Learn more at
HolyHeroes.com/Fatima

family to consecrate themselves to the Sacred Heart of Jesus shortly after his First Communion.[84]

Carlo knew well Jesus' promises revealed to Saint Margaret Mary between 1673 and 1675 for those who honor His Sacred Heart.

1. I will give them all the graces necessary in their state of life.
2. I will establish peace in their homes.
3. I will comfort them in all their afflictions.
4. I will be their secure refuge during life and, above all, in death.
5. I will bestow abundant blessings upon all their undertakings.
6. Sinners will find in My Heart the source and infinite ocean of mercy.
7. Lukewarm souls shall become fervent.
8. Fervent souls shall quickly mount to high perfection.
9. I will bless every place in which an image of My Heart is exposed and honored.
10. I will give to priests the gift of touching the most hardened hearts.
11. Those who shall promote this devotion shall have their names written in My Heart.
12. I promise you in the excessive mercy of My Heart that My all-powerful love will grant to all those who receive Holy Communion on the First Fridays in nine consecutive months the grace of final perseverance; they shall not die in My disgrace, nor without receiving their sacraments. My Divine Heart shall be their safe refuge in this last moment.

Not only did Carlo practice the First Friday Devotion, but he told everyone he knew about it. He also offered up sacrifices to Jesus' Sacred Heart to make up for the many sins committed by people every day against Jesus—not least of which was using Jesus' name in the place of cursing or damning something or someone, committing sacrileges with the Eucharist, or those who live with complete indifference to Jesus.[85]

Divine Mercy

During the Jubilee Year 2000, Pope Saint John Paul II instituted Divine Mercy Sunday, the first Sunday after Easter. Saint Faustina Kowalska wrote in her Diary that Jesus had told her: "The soul that will go to Confession and receive Holy Communion shall obtain complete forgiveness of sins and punishment. On that day all the divine floodgates through which graces flow are opened."[86]

Carlo was very intent on reciting the nine-day novena before Divine Mercy Sunday because he greatly feared ending up in Purgatory.[87]

Purgatory and Hell

Carlo's fear of Purgatory increased after reading the Treatise on Purgatory by Saint Catherine of Genoa. Carlo kept a notebook and wrote down the visions that various saints had on Hell and Purgatory. He would share this information with friends who didn't believe.

He also reflected often on the images of Hell as described by Saint Faustina—how, among all the torments of hell, souls are tormented by the particular sins of their senses. For example, those who did not control their tongues in life by what they would say or eat would be tormented on their tongues, or souls who did not control what they looked at with their eyes would be tormented in their eyes.[88]

Our Lady of Pompeii

The devotion to Our Lady of Pompeii centers on a miraculous painting of the Blessed Mother found at a basilica near the ruins of Pompeii in southern Italy. There have been so many miraculous cures associated with prayers to Our Lady of Pompeii that the painting is now studded with diamonds and gold from people who donated them in thanksgiving for answered prayers.

One day, in front of the Our Lady of Pompeii painting, Carlo prayed for the conversion of the mother of a dear friend of the family. She had not received the Eucharist nor gone to Confession for 30 years. Not long after his prayer, the woman returned to the sacraments. Carlos was so devoted to Our Lady of Pompeii that he consecrated himself to her seven times during his short life.[89]

Saint Francis of Assisi

One of the aspects of Saint Francis of Assisi that struck Carlo the most was his great humility. Carlo believed that humility was more than just being kind and charitable to others. He believed that true humility was something very difficult to attain—and that most of us are deluded about our humility because as soon as something happens in our life that we don't like, we are quick to get angry. Carlo was struck by the fact that Saint Francis fasted more than 200 days a year and yet was able to crisscross Italy on foot evangelizing thousands of people.[90]

Saint Anthony of Padua

Carlo was devoted to this beloved Italian saint. He often went to Padua, Italy, to pray at Saint Anthony's tomb.

He loved the story where Anthony converted a heretic in Rimini who did not believe in the real presence of Jesus in the Eucharist.

After a long debate, the heretic told Anthony that he would keep his donkey corralled for three days without food. Then the donkey would be released and shown food while Anthony would stand, holding the Eucharist in his hands. If the donkey ignored the food and bowed in front of the Eucharist, the heretic swore he would convert. Anthony accepted the challenge.

Three days later, in front of the entire town crowded into the piazza, Anthony held up a consecrated host in his hands. He called out, "Mule! Come here and show reverence to your Creator!" The donkey walked forward, ignored his master's food, and bowed down before Anthony and the Blessed Sacrament.[91]

Saint Michael, the Archangel

Saint Padre Pio often said that the best place to cure people possessed by demons was in the Grotto of Saint Michael the Archangel, which is near San Giovanni Rotondo, Italy. This cave is said to have an imprint on its wall of Saint Michael's wings.

According to tradition, Saint Michael appeared there in 493 A.D. It is one of the oldest shrines in Italy and a major Catholic pilgrimage site. When he appeared, Saint Michael said, "I am the guardian of this cave. ... That which is asked here in prayer will be fulfilled."

Carlo was so impressed by this sacred place that he began the habit of praying to the nine angelic choirs every day.[92]

The Last Things

Carlo often pondered the four "last things": death, judgment, Hell, and Heaven. He talked about these things at school so often that his schoolmates sometimes teased him, calling him a fanatic. Still, Carlo persisted, speaking fearlessly.

"If souls really run the risk of being damned, as many saints have given witness to, and also was confirmed by the apparitions of Fatima, I ask myself what is the reason why today nobody talks about Hell? Because it is something so terrible and frightening that it scares me just to think about it."[93]

Andrea Acutis, when remembering Carlo said, "My son lived an absolutely normal life, but he always had in mind that sooner or later he would die. Many times, when people would ask him about his future, he would say, 'Yes, if we will still be alive tomorrow or the day after that because I can't be sure how many years we will all live—the future is only known by God.'"[94]

Carlo understood that people must always be ready to stand before God, that all are called to live a moral life, and that both major and minor sins should be confessed right away so that one is always ready to stand before the Lord after death.

Confession

Carlo went to Confession every week, and he went to Bologna once a month to meet with his spiritual director, Father Ilio Carria. For Carlo, Reconciliation was like trying to fly in a hot air balloon. He had to let go of the weights of sin to fly up to God. If a person has committed a mortal sin, it is like their hot air balloon falling to the ground. Confession is the fire that helps the balloon to rise again.[95]

Carlo often pondered what happens to a soul who dies without having gone to Confession. One story from the life of Saint John Bosco (who lived in Italy 1815-1888) left an indelible mark on him. A fifteen-year-old boy (also named Carlo) knew Saint John Bosco and often said that he hoped to have the Saint at his bedside when it was his turn to die.

This boy fell gravely ill when Bosco was traveling and passed away. When Bosco returned from his travels, he went straight to Carlo's house. The saintly priest prayed fervently for Carlo to rise. Suddenly, Carlo sat up and told everyone about a terrible dream that he had where he was entering into a place of eternal flames, but a woman stopped him before he fell in.

This boy knew that he had omitted to confess one mortal sin during his last Confession. Bosco asked the boy to make his last Confession one more time without omitting anything. This he did. When Bosco asked him if he wished to stay on earth or go to Heaven, he answered, "Heaven."

"Therefore, we will see you in Heaven," Bosco said. The boy fell back in his bed and died peacefully.[96]

These and other similar stories convinced Carlo Acutis that many are ignorant of the dangers of dying with mortal sins on their souls. If people truly understood the risks they face, they would be more careful not to break God's commandments

Plenary Indulgences

Carlo understood that there are many ways to gain a plenary indulgence: adoring the Blessed Sacrament for at least half an hour, reciting the Rosary in church or with your family or community, and then going to Confession and receiving Holy Communion.

Carlo would often stop at a church to pray in Eucharistic adoration and then offer his indulgences to the poor souls in Purgatory.

Learn
"How to Make
A Holy Hour" at
HolyHeroes.com

and would run to Confession whenever they could.

Carlo believed that his two worst habits were laziness and eating too much. These were two defects he worked to conquer his whole life.[97]

Saint Padre Pio made a big impression on Carlo concerning laziness: During the winter of 1921 and 1922, the Capuchin priest often went to pray in the choir loft while the other friars were eating their dinner in the dining hall.

One night while he was praying, he heard a terrible crash coming from one of the church's side altars. Pio saw a young friar standing there. Pio asked him, "What are you doing here?"

The young friar said, "I am doing my Purgatory here. I was a seminary student in this convent, and I have to expiate my sins that I committed while I was here because I was not diligent in doing my chores in cleaning this church!"

Padre Pio discovered that the seminarian had died sixty years earlier, and his only sin had been to neglect his chores of cleaning the church. Padre Pio told his fellow friars, "Imagine how long and how hard Purgatory will be for those who did worse things than that!"[98]

The Cloistered Life

Another of Carlo's passions was visiting the great monasteries and shrines of Italy. The family often spent Sundays outside of Milan at the Abbey of Morimondo. Carlo loved the peace and tranquility of nature there.

He believed that cloistered monks and nuns were very important for the life of the Church because if they succeeded in carrying out their contemplative vocation, they could help many people who did not pray or know God by calling down graces from Heaven.[99]

"Happiness is when
your gaze focuses on God.
Sadness is when your gaze
is turned towards yourself."

—Carlo Acutis

Carlo's Final Act

In 2006, when Carlo was fifteen, many of his classmates came down with the flu. When he began to feel sick, on October 2, his parents assumed it was the same flu that was going around. While still at home, Carlo told his parents he was offering up his sufferings to God for the Pope and the Church so that he would not have to go to Purgatory but rather go directly to Heaven.

By October 8, Carlo's condition had deteriorated. He had blood in his urine and his parents realized that his sickness was much worse than the flu. They brought him to the De Marchi Clinic in Milan where he was diagnosed with M3 acute leukemia, which is the most aggressive type of blood cancer.

When the doctors told Carlo how serious the situation was, he did not cry. He turned to his parents and said, "Well, God just gave me a wake-up call."[100]

During this last week of Carlo's life, Antonia dreamed that Saint Francis of Assisi spoke to her. He said, "Your son Carlo will die very soon, but he will be considered very high in the Church."

She then saw Carlo in a very big church, very close to the ceiling, but she did not understand its meaning.[101]

Carlo told his mother, "Mama, I would like to leave the hospital, but I know that I will not be able to do so alive. I will give you signs, though, that I am with God."[102]

He also told her,

"I'm happy to die because I've lived my life without wasting even a minute of it doing things that wouldn't have pleased God."[103]

The doctors and nurses were struck by Carlo's serenity when he received his diagnosis and how he accepted his treatments. When they asked him how he felt, he told them with a smile that there were others who suffered more than he did. Carlo never complained, and he apologized for not being able to move because he was so tired.

While in the clinic, Carlo was in the intensive care unit. Doctors placed a plastic helmet on his head to help him breathe better. However, whenever he had to cough, he could not clear the cough well, which caused him great distress.

On October 9, Carlo was transferred to the San Gerardo di Monza Hospital in Milan, which specializes in blood diseases. Here, the hospital allowed Carlo's mother and grandmother to sleep in the room with him, which was a great comfort for the family.

The next day, Carlo requested the sacrament of the Anoint-

San Gerardo di Monza Hospital in Milan, Italy.

ing of the Sick and Holy Communion because he was certain he would soon die.

The following afternoon, Carlo went into a coma. Though he was given one last blood treatment that day, he ended up having a brain hemorrhage. The next morning, on October 12 at 6:45 a.m., Carlo's heart stopped beating. It was the vigil of the anniversary of the final apparition at Fatima.

Carlo had lived for only three days after his diagnosis.

After his death, Carlo's parents immediately went to see their pastor, Monsignor Gianfranco Poma.

"You know, Father, Carlo left us," they told him.

The pastor didn't even know that Carlo had been sick. At first, he misunderstood, thinking that Carlo had run away. Then his parents said, "No, the Lord took him away."

The shock of Carlo's death took his breath away.

"It was an unthinkable heartache," said Father Gianfranco.[104]

Carlo's parents were able to bring his body home for four days so that friends and family could see him for the last time. Just like Saint Padre Pio emanated a smell of roses, everyone noticed a strong smell of lilies coming from Carlo's body.[105]

Signs and Miracles

As soon as Carlo died, a virtual hurricane began. It was a hurricane of shock and grief, as well as the growing feeling that Carlo had truly been a Saint.

On the day of Carlo's funeral at Santa Maria Segreta, October 14, there were so many people in the church that an overflow crowd spilled out into the streets. Besides Carlo's classmates, there were many people that Carlo's parents didn't know at all—doormen, shopkeepers, and neighborhood men and women that Carlo had talked to through the years without his parents' knowledge. There were also homeless men and women. Italy's most important daily newspapers reported on the funeral and Carlo's life.[106]

"He was friends with everybody," said Antonia.[107]

The funeral ended at exactly noon and after the final prayer, the church bells began to ring furiously, as they always do at noon in many Italian towns. Yet, for those who attended the funeral, it seemed as if it was a sign that Carlo was indeed in Paradise.[108]

People began to claim Carlo was already interceding from Heaven for miracles at the funeral itself. A forty-five-year-old woman who attended the funeral had tried for years to conceive children but was never able to. She became pregnant after asking Carlo's intercession at his funeral Mass. Another woman who attended the funeral had cancer. She prayed to Carlo and discovered that she was healed.[109]

Another woman, an Indian Hindu, felt that she had received a special grace at the funeral to make peace with her granddaughter, with whom she had not spoken in years. She also felt the grace to convert to Catholicism and seek Baptism.[110]

Carlo's mother has received many stories of people who changed their lives because of Carlo's witness to the Faith. Many people have told Antonia that Carlo has appeared to them.[111]

Carlo's death transformed the lives of everyone in his school. Many parents testified that Carlo's death improved their relationship with their own children. Teenagers stopped taking their parents for granted as well. People began to think more about how their actions affect others. People were also more aware of how brief life is and how little time there is to do God's will during their lifetime.[112]

Many teenagers who knew Carlo came back to Mass after his death and others dedicated themselves to volunteering to help the poor. Many who knew him regularly ask for his intercession.

Predictions and Consolations

A few weeks after the funeral, Antonia woke up before dawn and heard a word in her mind: "testament." She ran to Carlo's room and looked around. Then she decided to turn on Carlo's computer, his favorite object in the house. She found a video Carlo had made of himself three months earlier. In the video he said, "When I weigh seventy kilograms (one hundred fifty-four pounds), I am destined to die."[113]

Carlo had grown to be six feet tall and one hundred fifty-four pounds. He had apparently predicted his own death. He had always said that life is a gift and time should not be wasted because we do not know when God will call us home.

Four years to the day after Carlo died, Antonia, at the age of forty-four, gave birth to twins—Francesca and Michele. Andrea and Antonia believe these children are a special grace from Carlo in Heaven.

A few years after Carlo died, he appeared in a dream to his mother saying, "I will be beatified soon and shortly after, canonized."[114]

Carlo's prayer overheard
by his parents a few days before
he was taken to the hospital:

**"I offer all the sufferings
that I will have to suffer,
to the Lord, for the Pope
and for the Church,
in order not to go to Purgatory
and go straight to Heaven."**

There was one who pleased God and was loved by Him,
and while living among sinners he was taken up.
He was caught up lest evil change his understanding
or guile deceive his soul.
For the fascination of wickedness obscures what is good,
and roving desire perverts the innocent mind.
Being perfected in a short time, he fulfilled long years;
for his soul was pleasing to the Lord,
therefore He took him quickly from
the midst of wickedness.

WISDOM 4:10–14

CONGREGATION FOR THE CAUSES OF SAINTS

MILAN
Beatification and Canonization
of the Servant of God
CARLO ACUTIS
Laity
(1991-2006)

DECREE ON VIRTUES

"Consummatus in short, explevit tempora multa"
(Being perfected in a short time, he fulfilled long years)
Wisdom 4:13

(Translation below from the Italian by the Author)

The reflection of the wise man of Israel is appropriately adapted to the Servant of God Carlo Acutis, who in just fifteen years reached the end of his life and the fullness of human and Christian perfection.

The Servant of God was born in London on May 3, 1991, to Andrea and Antonia Salzano and was brought to the baptismal font on May 18 in the church of Our Lady of Dolours in the British capital. From here in September of the same year he moved with his family to Milan. He received an excellent education in the family context and attended elementary school at some religious institutes, showing from early childhood a serene and affable temperament and an open and jovial character. But, above all, his spiritual profile was taking shape: his irrepressible desire to receive the sacrament of the Eucharist led him to ask in advance to receive First Holy Communion. Given his precocious maturity and spiritual preparation, his spiritual director granted him permission. To prepare well for meeting with the Lord, Carlo studied and assimilated the Catechism. Thus, on June 16, 1998, he received his First

Communion, and on May 24, 2003, he was administered the Sacrament of Confirmation.

Often, during the holidays, he spent a lot of time with his family in Assisi, where he felt at ease, progressively reaching a profound spiritual maturity, following in the footsteps of Franciscan spirituality, dedicating himself with particular fervor to marked Eucharistic piety and intense Marian devotion. After the middle school, he enrolled as a fourteen-year-old the a classical high school called Leone XIII Institute in Milan, acquiring, among other things, a rare competence in the IT field, so much so that he designed a new website promoting community service for his high school and shortly afterwards a website for the Pontificia Academia Cultorum Martyrum.

During the years of the school process, although his studies were demanding, he spontaneously decided to dedicate part of his time to preparing children for Confirmation, teaching catechism in his parish of Santa Maria Segreta. Due to his warm personality and sense of humor, he was always the center of attention of his friends. He helped others with computer problems and helped them to become familiar with IT programs. There are many certificates of recognition of his computer skills and his complete willingness to make them available to his classmates and anyone in need, including family members. His obedience to parents and educators was admirable. In them, he saw reflected the will of the Father. On the other hand, he had a faith that attracted others and was contagious.

The center of his spirituality was the daily encounter with the Lord in the Eucharist. Carlo often said: "The Eucharist is my highway to Heaven!". After his First Communion, he began to attend Mass every day. In imitation of the little shepherds of Fatima, he offered small sacrifices for those who do not love the Lord. Thus, he carried out a precious work of apostolate among his schoolmates and friends and, as a true apostle of the Eucharist, he chose to use his IT talent to design and create an international exhibition on "Eucharistic miracles": a large photographic exhibit on the main Eucharistic wonders that have occurred over the centuries in various countries of the world.

Carlo followed Christ fully and bore witness to the Gospel even in difficult environments and in the midst of people belonging to other religions. He never discriminated against or excluded anyone. Although belonging to a very wealthy family, he never showed attachment to material goods. On the contrary, he shared them with the poor. Carlo's charity towards the poor, the homeless, immigrants and the marginalized was exemplary. His main objective was to evangelize people in order to lead them back to God. His mastery in using the computer make him an example for the not only lawful, but even fruitful and good use of the internet and social networks.

Carlo prayed the Rosary daily and consecrated himself to the Virgin Mary to renew his affection for her and to implore her support. In his spiritual life, awareness for the Last Things was always present, with their prospect of eternal life. For him ultra-earthly realities were habitual, daily realities, as was his love and respect for the Church, the Pope and his magisterium, bishops and priests: he prayed for all and entrusted everyone to the Sacred Heart of Jesus.

In the first days of October 2006, he suffered from a serious illness, initially judged as a simple flu, and subsequently diagnosed as type M3 leukemia, considered the most aggressive form of leukemia. He kept his serenity and joviality until the end, even in the most critical moments of evil, by now certain of the next encounter with God, edifying those around him with his behavior and with his words. First admitted to the De Marchi Clinic in Milan and then to the San Gerardo Hospital in Monza, he was diagnosed with brain death on the evening of 11 October 2006, while his heart stopped beating in the early hours of the following day. Two days later the funeral was celebrated in the church of Santa Maria Segreta. The body was initially buried in the family tomb in Ternengo (Biella),

By virtue of its reputation for holiness, the Diocesan Inquiry was held at the Ecclesiastical Curia of Milan from 12 October 2013 to 24 November 2016, the legal validity of which was recognized by this Congregation with a decree of 26 May 2017. While preparing the Positio , it was discussed according to the usual procedure whether this Servant of God exercised the virtues in a heroic degree. With a positive outcome, the Peculiar Congress of Theological Consultors was held on April 17, 2018. The Cardinal Fathers and Bishops in the Ordinary Session of 3 July 2018, presided over by me, Cardinal Angelo Amato, recognized that the Servant of God exercised the theological, cardinal and annexed virtues to a heroic degree.

(Official Latin Decree Text)

Facta demum de hisce omnibus rebus Summo Pontifici Francisco per subscriptum Cardinalem Praefectum accurate relatione,

Sanctitas Sua, vota Congregationis de Causis Sanctorum excipiens rataque habens, hodierno die declaravit: Constare de virtutibus theologalibus Fide, Spe et Caritate tum in Deum tum in proximum, nec cardinalibus Prudentia, Iustitia, Temperantia et Fortitudine, iisque adnexis, in gradu heroico, Servi Dei Caroli Acutis, Christifidelis Laici, in casu et ad effectum de quo agitur.

Hoc autem decretum publici iuris fieri et in acta Congregationis de Causis Sanctorum Summus Pontifex referri mandavit.

Datum Romae, die 5 mensis Iulii a. D. 2018.

ANGELO Card. AMATO, SDB
Prefect

+MARCELLO BARTOLUCCI
Archbishop Tit. of Bevagna
Secretary

Matheus Vianna was miraculously cured through Carlo's intercession.

Carlo's Life after Death

The Miracle

In order for the Vatican to officially approve Carlo's beatification, at least one miracle had to have occurred which could be definitively proven as being caused by Carlo's intercession.

Seven years after Carlo's passing, exactly such a miracle happened in Brazil. A Brazilian priest named Father Marcelo Tenorio had learned of the many miracles that were being reported since Carlo's death. (The day Carlo died, October 12, happens to be the feast day of Our Lady of Aparecida, Brazil's patroness.) While Father Tenorio was visiting Assisi one year, he had the honor of meeting Antonia. He asked her if his parish could have a relic of her son, and she later sent him a piece of cloth from the pajamas that Carlo was wearing when he was in the hospital.

Every year, Father Tenorio would display Carlo's relic after the celebration of Our Lady of Aparecida's feast day so the people in his parish could venerate it. In 2013, a four-year-old boy named Matheus Vianna, who was born with a malformed pancreas, came to pray to Carlo with his mother and grandparents.

Because of the difficulties caused by his pancreas, Matheus was unable to eat any solid foods. As a result, he had become dangerously weak and malnourished.

"He used to vomit almost constantly, two minutes after eating anything. We had to give him special formula so that he could retain at least some nutrients," Matheus' mother said.* Only a transplant could save the child, but he was too weak for surgery. Doctors told Ms. Vianna that Matheus would die before the age of five.

"That day, Matheus saw the line of people standing to venerate Carlo's relic and he asked me what they were doing. I told him we could pray to Carlo for anything, if we wanted to, because he was in Heaven," Ms. Vianna said. Matheus leapt out of his grandfather's lap, went up to the relic, kissed it, and said a prayer out loud, using only two words: "Stop vomiting!"

After the Mass, Matheus was unusually joyful—and he was hungry! When he got home, he ate beef and some French fries, and he did not become sick.

"Since that day, I knew he was cured because of Carlo," Matheus' mother said. "The change was too drastic and too sudden."

Matheus began to gain weight, and when he went to his medical appointments, an ultrasound examination confirmed that his pancreas had been fully healed.

"One doctor said that he now had a textbook pancreas, an organ that is so perfect that it looks unreal," Ms. Vianna said. Another doctor told her that he was surprised that "Matheus' surgery had left no scars," even though he had not had any surgery.

Vatican experts thoroughly examined all of the evidence and they concluded that Matheus' healing was indeed a miracle that could not be explained by science.

Today [2022] Matheus is twelve years old, and thanks to the miracle attributed to the intercession of Blessed Carlo, he lives a normal life.

For all new followers of Blessed Carlo Acutis, Ms. Vianna has a clear message: "What most defines Carlo is not being an ordinary young man in sneakers, carrying a backpack on his back, but his love for the Eucharist. What makes him extraordinary is his love, his unusual love. Carlo brings an explosion of love and liveliness to the Church."

*The most detailed account of the miracle can be found here: Philipe Domingues, https://www.americamagazine.org/faith/2020/11/20/blessed-carlo-acutis-saint-relics-millennial-miracle, November 20, 2020.

CONGREGATION FOR THE CAUSES OF SAINTS

Venerable
CARLO ACUTIS
(1991-2006)

THE MIRACLE

(Translation below from the Italian by the Author)

In view of his beatification, the Postulator presented the presumed miraculous cure of a child to the Congregation for the Causes of Saints.

The event occurred on October 12, 2013, in Campo Grande, Brazil. The little one, since his birth in 2010, suffered from significant disorders of the digestive system. In 2012, a clinical examination revealed a rare congenital anatomical anomaly of the pancreas. Due to this pathology, the child's life was characterized by poor growth and difficulty in feeding. Several times he was hospitalized for dehydration and inflammatory processes. Only surgery could have eliminated the problem.

The surgery, however, was never carried out. In 2013, after the little sick boy touched a relic of the Venerable Carlo Acutis, a surprising change was recorded and the resumption of normal body-weight growth. Clinical tests, carried out in the following years, revealed that the pancreas no longer presented the initial anatomical problem, without any surgical intervention being performed, as would have been necessary to eliminate functional disorders. The initiative of the invocation was taken by the parish priest of S. Sebastiano in Campo Grande and by the child's parents. On the occasion of the anniversary of the death of the Venerable Servant of God, the parish priest had organized the celebration of a Mass. Meanwhile, the sick man's mother had started a novena to ask for the healing of her son. In addition to family members, many acquaintances and parishioners joined in the invocations addressed to the Venerable. The prayer was made in a context of faith that involved an entire parish community. The healing of the child took place during the Holy Mass, immediately after the kiss of the relic.

The chronological concomitance and the connection between the invocation to the Ven. Servant of God and the healing of the child, who subsequently enjoyed good health and was able to manage a normal relational life, is evident.

On the healing, considered miraculous, the Diocesan Inquiry was investigated at the Curia of Campo Grande in Brazil from 24 April to 12 June 2018, the legal validity of which was recognized by this Congregation with a decree of 15 March 2019. The Medical Council of the Dicastery in the session of November 14, 2019 acknowledged that the healing was rapid, complete and lasting, inexplicable in the light of current medical knowledge. The Peculiar Congress of Theological Consultors was held on 17 December 2019. The Ordinary Session of the Cardinals and Bishops took place on 4 February 2020, presided over by Cardinal Angelo Becciu.

Relics of Saints

Relics are physical objects that have a direct association with the Saints or Jesus. There are three classes of relics:

First class relics are from the body of a Saint *(often fragments of bone)*. **Second class relics** are personal items a Saint used, such as clothing. **Third class relics** are items a Saint touched or that have been touched to a first, second, or another third class relic of a Saint.

Holy Scripture in both the Old Testament and the New Testament provides numerous examples of God exercising His power through relics, especially for healing.

When the corpse of a man was touched to the bones of the prophet Elisha, the man came back to life.

Elisha died and was buried. Now Moabite raiders used to enter the country every spring. Once while some Israelites were burying a man, suddenly they saw a band of raiders; so they threw the man's body into

Elisha's tomb. When the body touched Elisha's bones, the man came to life and stood up on his feet. (2 Kings 13:20-21)

People would bring the sick to the streets so that when Saint Peter walked by they might be healed.

Now many signs and wonders were done among the people by the hands of the Apostles. ...so that they even carried out the sick into the streets, and laid them on beds and pallets, that as Peter came by at least his shadow might fall on some of them. (Acts 5:12-15)

Cloths touched to Saint Paul were then touched to the sick to heal them.

And God did extraordinary miracles by the hands of Paul, so that handkerchiefs or aprons were carried away from his body to the sick, and diseases left them and the evil spirits came out of them. (Acts 19:11-12)

The power to heal through the physical object (the relic) comes from God. God chooses to use the relics of Saints as His tools to work miracles in order to draw our attention to the Saints as our intercessors who are with Him in Heaven and as models for how to live our lives on earth.

—*The Publisher*

Carlo's beatification ceremony at Santa Maria Maggiore in Assisi, Italy.

Beatification

Exhumation and Celebration

The Church declared Carlo Venerable on July 5, 2018, and he was beatified on October 10, 2020, in Assisi. Before the beatification, there was a seventeen-day celebration leading up to the ceremony.

Carlo's tomb was opened so that his body could be venerated through a glass window where people could see him dressed in jeans and sneakers. After the beatification, Carlo's tomb was closed.

Since Carlo's death, pilgrimages to Assisi have skyrocketed. Thousands of people visit Saint Francis of Assisi's tomb every year, but now the numbers have grown exponentially for pilgrims who visit Carlo's tomb, which is in Assisi's Shrine of Saint Mary Major.

In the first three weeks of October 2020 alone, despite COVID-19 regulations, more than forty-one thousand people visited Carlo's tomb.

> For those who cannot visit Carlo's tomb,
> there is a direct webcam on his tomb:
> **https://www.mariavision.it/santuario-spogliazione-assisi**

The beatification ceremony was streamed live on Facebook and followed by 569,000 people. People from around the world watched the Mass live on Catholic television networks like EWTN.

Antonia has said publicly that had it not been for her Catholic faith, which was inspired and increased by her son Carlo, she would not have been able to accept his death. Today, Antonia and Andrea Acutis live happily, knowing that Carlo's life has become a beacon of hope and light for countless millions of young people.

There are so many requests for the Acutis family to give talks about Carlo that they cannot keep up. It does, however, give them great joy to see the positive effect of Carlo's life on others. His parents believe that Carlo's death, illness, and short life were all by God's design — and that God had chosen Carlo to be an example for young people in this period of history.[115]

"There have been many spiritual conversions. Many people who have come back to the Church," said Antonia. "Only by the hand of God has this been possible."[116]

What Comes Next?

How a "Blessed" becomes a "Saint"

"As well as reassuring us that the Servant of God lives in Heaven in communion with God, miracles constitute the divine confirmation of the judgment expressed by the ecclesiastical authority on a his/her virtuous life."

—Pope Benedict XVI,
*Letter to the Participants of the Plenary Session
of the Congregation for the Causes of Saints,*
April 24, 2006

When someone is beatified, the Church calls him or her "Blessed." When someone is canonized, the Church then calls him or her a "Saint."

What is the difference, however, considering that for beatification the evidence of a miracle proving that a person is in Heaven is required?

The answer that the Church is awaiting a final "divine confirmation" that *God desires the entire Universal Church* to venerate a person *publicly* everywhere.

For each step, the Church waits for God to make His wishes known through miracles.

The first miracle is God's initial confirmation that He desires at least some of the faithful to venerate the Blessed as a model for a virtuous life and as an intercessor in Heaven to whom they can

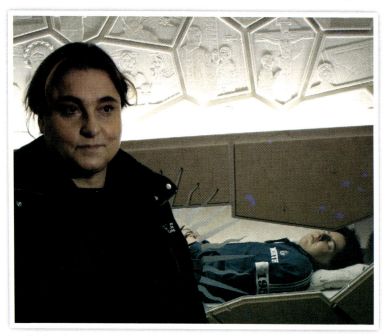

Carlo's mother Antonia stands in front of Carlo's tomb at Santa Maria Maggiore in Assisi, Italy.

turn for divine aid. The second miracle is His final confirmation that now He desires the entire Church to celebrate what He has done through the life of one of His creatures.

Beatification permits public veneration in places closely associated with his or her life (such as in a diocese or other geographic area or in a religious community most closely associated with the Blessed). Of course, we can all privately pray to a Blessed knowing that he or she is in Heaven and can hear and respond to our prayers (perhaps with another miracle!).

Being declared a "Saint" opens up that public celebration to the entire Church. It also means that churches can be dedicated to the Saint without special permission from the Vatican.

Being declared "Blessed" *permits* the faithful in the Church to venerate a person; being declared a "Saint" *requires* that a person be venerated in the Church's liturgy and especially with a Mass in his or her honor.

What is required for a "Blessed" to become a "Saint"? Another miracle through his or her intercession—*after* the beatification.

—The Publisher

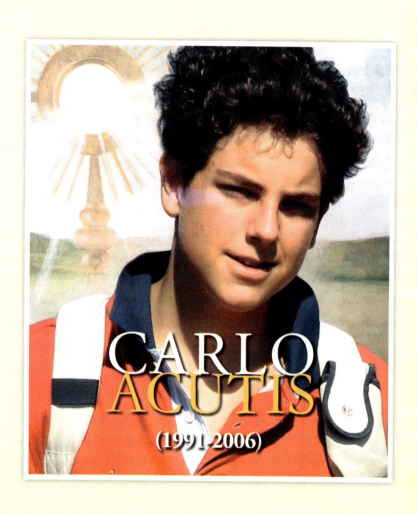

Official Prayer For the Canonization of Blessed Carlo Acutis

Oh Father, Who has given us the ardent testimony of the young Blessed Carlo Acutis, who made the Eucharist the core of his life and the strength of his daily commitments so that everybody may love You above all else, let him soon be counted among the Saints in Your Church.

Confirm my faith, nurture my hope, strengthen my charity, in the image of young Carlo who, growing in these virtues, now lives with You. Grant me the grace that I need [state intention].

I trust in You, Father, and Your Beloved Son Jesus, in the Virgin Mary, our Dearest Mother, and in the intercession of Your Blessed Carlo Acutis.

Our Father, Hail Mary, Glory Be

Imprimatur in Curia Archiepiscopali Mediolanensi
6 October 2014, +Angelo Mascheroni

(top) Santa Maria Maggiore in Assisi, Italy. (bottom) Santuario della Spogliazione (the Shrine of the Stripping)

Post-Script

Reliquary containing a portion of Carlo's heart.

The recognition of Carlo's particular type of holiness—lived within the context of the 21st Century—has gained momentum year after year. People began to pray for his intercession immediately after his death, with many favors and miracles being reported to and documented by the Acutis family since that time.

Carlo was first buried in Piedmont, Italy, after his death—close to where the Acutis family lived. In January 2007, his body was transferred to Assisi, which is where he had requested to be buried prior to dying.

In 2009, the first oratory—or small chapel—was established in Carlo's honor in Assisi by the Bishop of Assisi, Domenico Sorrentino. It was located right next to Santa Maria Maggiore in Assisi.

In January 2019, the body of Carlo was exhumed in Assisi.

Though his body was found to be in a very good state, it was not, however, incorrupt as some saints bodies have been found to be. Carlo's face was reconstructed with a silicone mask prior to his beatification. This process—according to Bishop Sorrentino—was carried out with the utmost respect, love, and honor. Also, during this time, a part of Carlo's heart was removed, which was exhibited as a relic during his beatification.

On April 6, 2019, Carlo's body was moved to its permanent place inside the Church of Santa Maria Maggiore in Assisi in a chapel called the Shrine of the Stripping. This is where St. Francis of Assisi rid himself of all his wealthy clothes and returned them to his father. Carlo's tomb remains there to this day.

Carlo was beatified on October 10, 2020, just two days before the 14th anniversary of his death. During the beatification Mass, Carlo's parents and younger sister and brother processed behind the relic of his heart.

Today, Carlo's body is covered in marble—and can be visited in Assisi. Pilgrims come from all over the world to pray at his tomb. By October 11, 2021, the diocese of Assisi estimated that 117,000 pilgrims had already visited Carlo's tomb.

Since the beatification, the Acutis family waits for another miracle to be approved. Few people doubt that Carlo won't make it to the next stage of canonization.

For millennial Catholics—especially those involved with computer programming and technology—there is already a friend in Heaven ready to inspire and intercede for them.

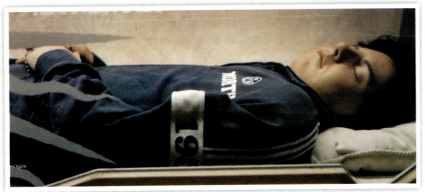

(top) Beatification Mass in Assisi, Italy. (middle and bottom) Blessed Carlo Acutis Chapel & Tomb

Carlo's Sayings

"The Eucharist is my highway to Heaven."

Carlo used to say this because he believed that receiving the Eucharist with reverence was the fastest way to reach Heaven. His whole life centered on the Eucharist because he wanted to be in communion with Jesus. Receiving the Eucharist, for him, meant being with his best friend.

"Our aim has to be the infinite and not the finite. The infinite is our homeland."

"We have always been expected in Heaven."

"All of us are born as originals, but most of us die as photocopies."
What Carlo meant by this is that we are all unique. We all receive gifts from God. We have potential from the beginning which unfortunately often gets lost along the way because we try to become like everyone else, conforming ourselves to others. Thus, we often lose our gifts and identity as we strive to become just like everybody else in order to "fit in." We do not realize that we are all unique and unrepeatable children of God. All of us have the capacity within ourselves to be holy.

"My goal is to get to Heaven."

"Sadness is when we are turned towards ourselves. Happiness is when we turn towards God."

"In order for a hot air balloon to rise, it has to let go of weights. This is what happens when you go to confession, you must get rid of venial and mortal sins in order to get closer to God and rise up."

"The more Eucharist we receive, the more we become like Jesus so that on this earth we have a foretaste of Heaven."
Carlo believed that the sacraments were a fountain of mercy that help us to carry our sufferings.

"God has written for each of us a unique and unrepeatable story – but He has left us free to write the end of the story."

"Happiness in this life will only be partial. Christ promises full happiness in Heaven. The compass of how to get there is Scripture, to guide and orient you in daily life like an anchor – and to find answers to your problems."

"I will become what in God's mind I already am."

"The Rosary is the shortest stairway to reach Heaven."

"A life is really beautiful only if one loves God above every other thing, and his neighbor as himself."

"Criticizing the Church means criticizing ourselves. The Church is the dispenser of treasures for our salvation"

"The only thing we have to really fear is sin."

"Why do human beings worry so much about the beauty of their own bodies and they do not worry about the beauty of their own souls?"

"Not me, but God."

"Not love of self, but the glory of God."

"To always be united to Jesus – this is my life's plan"
    Carlo wrote this when he was only seven years old.

"What does it serve man to win a thousand battles if he is not able to conquer himself?"

"Holiness is not a process of addition, but subtraction, the less I am, the more I give space to God."

"After the Holy Eucharist, the Holy Rosary is the strongest weapon to fight the Devil."

"Happiness is when your gaze focuses on God. Sadness is when your gaze is turned towards yourself."

"If God possesses our heart, then we possess the infinite."

"When you stand in front of the sun, you get sunburned. When you stand before Jesus in the Eucharist, you become a Saint."

Carlo's "Kit" for Becoming a Saint

In order to help the children in his catechism classes, Carlo created a "kit" to help them become Saints.

This Kit consisted of just eight things
1. Becoming a Saint—You have to want this with all of your heart and if you don't desire it, you have to pray for it constantly to God.
2. Try to go every day to Mass and to receive Holy Communion.
3. Remember to recite the Rosary every day.
4. Read a little bit of the Bible every day.
5. If you can, stay a few moments every day in Eucharistic Adoration in front of the tabernacle where Jesus is really present, and you will see your level of holiness increase considerably.
6. If you can, go to Confession every week—even if just to confess your venial sins.
7. Make mortifications/sacrifices and renunciations frequently to Our Lord and Our Lady to help others.
8. Ask your Guardian Angel continuously for help so that he becomes your best friend.

Timeline

May 3, 1991: Carlo Acutis is born in London

May 18, 1991: Carlo is baptized at Our Lady of Dolours Catholic Church in London. Both sets of grandparents are present, as well as his great grandmother Adriana, and his aunt Adriana.

September 8, 1991: Carlo and his parents return to Milan.

June 16, 1998: Carlo receives his First Communion at the Convent of the Romite Sisters of Saint Ambrose in Perego, Italy.

May 24, 2003: Carlo receives the Sacrament of Confirmation in his parish church of Santa Maria Segreta in Milan, Italy.

October 2, 2006: Carlo becomes ill with what appears to be flu.

October 8, 2006: Carlo's condition continues to deteriorate, so he is taken to De Marchi Clinic in Milan. He is diagnosed with M3 acute leukemia, considered the most aggressive form of the disease.

October 9, 2006: Carlo is transferred to San Gerardo Hospital in Monza, Italy.

October 10, 2006: Carlo requests and receives the Sacrament of Anointing of the Sick and Holy Communion, feeling that he will die soon.

October 11, 2006: Carlo falls into a coma.

October 12, 2006: At 6:45 am, Carlo dies.

October 14, 2006: Carlo's funeral Mass is held at Santa Maria Segreta Church in Milan.

October 12, 2010: Antonia Acutis, Carlo's mother, gives birth to twins exactly four years after his death.

October 12, 2012: The Cause for Carlo's Beatification and Canonization is opened in the Diocese of Milan, and he is named a Servant of God.

May 13, 2013: The Holy See declares *"Nihil Obstat"* (nothing obstructs) the Cause of Servant of God Carlo Acutis, giving approval for the investigation into his life to move forward.

October 12, 2013: A four year old child, Matheus Vianna, is cured of a rare congenital pancreatic deformity after kissing a relic of

Servant of God Carlo Acutis during Holy Mass at San Sebastiano Church in Campo Grande, Brazil. His mother had also prayed a novena for his cure to Servant of God Carlo Acutis.

November 24, 2016: The diocesan investigation of the Cause for Servant of God Carlo Acutis is concluded and the Positio completed for forwarding to the Congregation for the Causes of Saints.

May 26, 2017: The Congregation for the Causes of Saints accepts the diocesan *Positio*.

April 24-June 12, 2018: The Diocese of Campo Grande investigates the miraculous cure of Matheus Vianna.

July 3, 2018: The Congregation for the Causes of Saints concludes that Servant of God Carlo Acutis lived a life of Heroic Virtue.

July 5, 2018: Pope Francis confirms the Decree of Heroic Virtue of Servant of God Carlo Acutis, declaring him Venerable.

January 23, 2019: The body of Venerable Carlo Acutis is exhumed for transfer from his original place of burial.

March 15, 2019: The Congregation for the Causes of Saints accepts the diocesan investigation of the miraculous cure of Matheus Vianna through the intercession of Venerable Carlo Acutis.

April 6, 2019: The body of Venerable Carlo Acutis is moved to the Shrine of the Renunciation in Assisi, Italy.

November 14, 2019: The Vatican's Medical Council of the Congregation for the Causes of Saints approves the miraculous cure of Matheus Vianna as being rapid, complete, and lasting, and medically inexplicable, thereby attributed to the intercession of Venerable Carlo Acutis.

October 10, 2020: Blessed Carlo Acutis is beatified in Assisi, Italy.

October 15, 2020: A parish is established in the Archdiocese of Birmingham, England, under the patronage of Blessed Carlo Acutis.

How to Learn More

CARLO'S OFFICIAL WEBSITE

www.carloacutis.com

CARLO'S CATHOLIC EXHIBITS & WEBSITES

Carlo's Eucharistic Miracles website:
www.miracolieucaristici.org/en/liste/list.html

Carlo's Marian Apparitions website:
www.themarianapparitions.org
  In 2014, Carlo's parents finished this exhibit that Carlo had begun in 2006. It has traveled to the US, Philippines, and throughout Europe and South America.

Carlo's Angels and Demons exhibit:
www.carloacutis.net/pages/angeli/index.html
  For this free exhibit send an e-mail to *info@carloacutis.com*

Carlo's Heaven, Hell, and Purgatory exhibit:
www.carloacutis.net/InfernoPurgatorioParadiso/
  For this free exhibit send an e-mail to *info@carloacutis.com*

PRAYER REQUESTS

Send your prayer requests for Carlo in Heaven to:
www.carloacutis.com/en/association/richieste-di-preghiera

BOOKS ABOUT CARLO ACUTIS & MIRACLES

Carlo Acutis: The First Millennial Saint
Nicola Gori, translated by Daniel Gallagher
 Written by the postulator for Carlo's Cause, this book includes many observations from those who knew Carlo as well as facts about his life and spiritual interests uncovered in the investigation which culminated in his beatification.

A Millennial in Paradise: Carlo Acutis
Will Conquer
 A fast read with questions at the end of each chapter providing thoughts and insights into how Carlo's example can impact your own life.

The Eucharistic Miracles of the World
Catalogue of the Vatican International Exhibition
 This is the catalog of the exhibit created by Carlo! A great resource for every home—for hours of contemplation and wonder!

Eucharistic Miracles
Joan Carroll Cruz
 This book documents 36 Eucharistic Miracles from 800 AD up to the present day, with hundreds of photos and astounding details of the scientific investigations into them.

Holy Mysteries! 12 Investigations into Extraordinary Cases
Sophie de Mullenheim, Solenne & Thomas; translated by Janet Chevrier
 For ages 9 & up and colorfully illustrated throughout, this book details twelve mysteries which are visible today, from the Shroud of Turin to the spring at Lourdes to the bones of Saint Peter and more. Kids love this book!

For these and more visit
HolyHeroes.com/Carlo
or call 1-855-Try2B-Holy (1-855-879-2246).

Helping You Bring the Joy of the Faith to Your Family

Get your Glory Stories® Volume 17, Audio CD today!

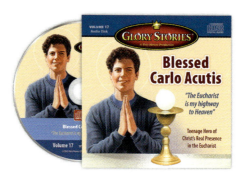

Blessed Carlo Acutis: *"The Eucharist is my highway to Heaven."*

Children (and adults) will be astonished and inspired by this audio drama! They will love Carlo's joy in the power of prayer, his example of how to be a big brother (surprising—and miraculous!), and his zeal to share the truths of the Faith in the 21st century.

Mom & Dad: Carlo's mother corresponded with our author to give us quotes and examples of how Carlo addressed issues faced by your kids today!

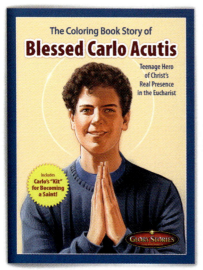

Includes Carlo's Kit for How to Become a Saint!

Carlo's story told in 32 beautiful coloring pages

Order online at **HolyHeroes.com/Carlo**
or call 1-855-Try2B-Holy (1-855-879-2246)

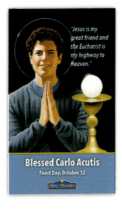

Available in 5-packs so you have plenty to share!

Blessed Carlo Acutis Prayer Cards
Help spread the word and celebrate this amazing teenager!

These large prayer cards (3"x 5") feature Blessed Carlo's "Kit" for How to Become a Saint. Remember to celebrate Blessed Carlo's Feast Day on October 12th!

Blessed Carlo Acutis Coloring Book
Teenage Hero of Christ's Real Presence in the Eucharist!

A great companion to the Audio CD—so your kids can color while they listen!

Endnotes

1 Nicola Gori, Eucharistia: La Mia Autostrada per il Cielo (Milan, Italy: Edizioni San Paolo, 2007), 28.
2 Ibid., p. 31
3 Ibid., p. 29
4 Ibid., p.29
5 Ibid., p.29
6 Mathilde De Robien – Cecilia Zinicola, "What Carlo Acutis' nanny taught him – and us," Aleteia, November 07, 2020.
7 Email interview with Acutis family, April 16, 2021.
8 Interview with Antonia Acutis, June 18, 2020.
9 Ibid., interview Acutis
10 Ibid., interview Acutis
11 Ibid., interview Acutis
12 Email interview with Acutis family, April 16, 2020
13 Gori, p. 35
14 Ibid., p. 35
15 Ibid., p. 35
16 Paola Ronconi, "Carlo Acutis: The Boy of Miracles," Communion and Liberation Online, October 10, 2020

17 Gori, p. 37
18 Nicola Gori, "Carlo Acutis: The First Millenial Saint," Florida Catholic Media, June 30, 2021.
19 Gori, p. 32
20 Ibid., p. 32
21 Gori, p. 40
22 Gori, p.65
23 Interview with Antonia Acutis
24 Gori, p. 66
25 Gori, p. 62
26 Gori, p. 37
27 Gori, p. 131
28 Gori, p. 64
29 Interview with Flavia Maria Zauli, cousin of Carlo Acutis in Vatican TV documentary "My Highway to Heaven: Carlo Acutis and the Eucharist" (Office of Communications, Rome)
30 Gori, p.62
31 Gori, p.64
32 Paola Bergamini, "It is Nothing more than Raising your Gaze up," Communion and Liberation Online, February 1st, 2014.
33 Interview with Msgr. Gianfranco Poma, pastor of Carlo Acutis at Santa Maria Segreta in Milan in Vatican TV documentary "My Highway to Heaven: Carlo Acutis and the Eucharist" (Office of Communications, Rome)
34 Gori, p.90
35 Interview with Flavia Maria Zauli, cousin of Carlo Acutis in Vatican TV documentary "My Highway to Heaven: Carlo Acutis and the Eucharist" (Office of Communications, Rome)
36 Interview with Nicola Gori, postulator for the cause of

canonization of Carlo Acutis, June 19, 2020

37 Gori, p.69, p.116, p.132

38 Gori, p.77

39 Interview with Gori

40 Interview with Antonia Acutis

41 Gori, p.76

42 Gori, p.47

43 Interview with Antonia Acutis

44 Vatican TV documentary "My Highway to Heaven: Carlo Acutis and the Eucharist" (Office of Communications, Rome)

45 Interview with Antonia Acutis

46 Gori, p.65

47 From official Carlo Acutis website: www.carloacutis.com

48 Gori, p.39

49 Interview with Federico Oldani, middle school friend of Carlo Acutis in Vatican TV documentary "My Highway to Heaven: Carlo Acutis and the Eucharist" (Office of Communications, Rome)

50 Gori, p.47

51 Gori, p.45

52 Interview with Antonia Acutis, June 18, 2020

53 Interview with Flavia Maria Zauli, cousin of Carlo Acutis in Vatican TV documentary "My Highway to Heaven: Carlo Acutis and the Eucharist" (Office of Communications, Rome)

54 Interview with Rajesh Mohur, housekeeper for Acutis family in Vatican TV documentary "My Highway to Heaven: Carlo Acutis and the Eucharist" (Office of Communications, Rome)

55 Angela Mengis Palleck ,"Carlo Acutis: Millenial Generation has a Blessed," Vatican News, October 10, 2020.

56 Ibid.

57 Gori, p.57
58 Ibid.
59 Ibid.
60 Ibid.
61 Gori, p.61
62 Interview with Antonia Acutis
63 Ibid.
64 Ibid.
65 Ibid.
66 From the website created by Carlo Acutis: www.miracolieucaristici.org
67 Ibid.
68 From email interview with the Acutis family, April 16, 2020
69 Ibid.
70 Interview with Antonia Acutis
71 Gori, p.54
72 Gori, p.52
73 Gori, p.51
74 Gori, p.53
75 Gori, p.55
76 Gori, p.55
77 Gori, p.56
78 Interview with Antonia Acutis
79 Gori, p.116
80 Gori, p.132
81 Gori, p.136
82 Gori, p.133
83 Ibid.
84 Gori, p.123

85 Gori, p.124
86 Diary of Faustina Kowalska, #699
87 Gori, p.118
88 Gori, p.120
89 Gori, p.117
90 Gori, p.70
91 Gori, p.75
92 Gori, p.115
93 Gori, p.79
94 Interview with Antonia Acutis
95 Vatican TV documentary "My Highway to Heaven: Carlo Acutis and the Eucharist" (Office of Communications, Rome) Rome)
96 Gori, p.100
97 Gori, p.65
98 Gori, p.112
99 Vatican TV documentary "My Highway to Heaven: Carlo Acutis and the Eucharist" (Office of Communications, Rome)
100 Gori, p.142
101 Email interview with Acutis family
102 Milena Castigli, "Carlo Acutis L'Influencer di Dio," In Terris, August 29, 2021
103 Corinna Turner, "Carlo Acutis: His Life and Legacy," Catholic Herald, October 9, 2020.
104 Interview with Msgr. Gianfranco Poma, Vatican TV documentary "My Highway to Heaven: Carlo Acutis and the Eucharist" (Office of Communications, Rome)
105 Gori, p.145
106 Interview with Nicola Gori

107 Interview with Antonia Acutis
108 Gori, p.145
109 Interview with Antonia Acutis
110 Gori, p.84
111 Email interview with Acutis family
112 Gori, p.49
113 Stefano Lorenzetto, "Carlo Acutis e' beato: La madre 'Vi racconto il suo miracolo'," Corriere Della Sera, October 10, 2020.
114 Ibid.
115 Interview with Nicola Gori
116 Interview with Antonia Acutis

About the Author

Sabrina Arena Ferrisi has been working in the field of Catholic journalism since the year 2000. She worked in Rome from 2000 to 2004 covering Vatican news for various American Catholic newspapers, including *Our Sunday Visitor*, the *National Catholic Register* and the *Catholic World Report*, as well as for the radio program Radio Maria. She was the senior staff writer for *Legatus Magazine* for 14 years and currently writes freelance for the *National Catholic Register* and *Aleteia*. From 2019 to 2020, Sabrina covered the activities of the Holy See at the United Nations for EWTN Nightly News. She has a bachelors in political science and international relations from Brown University and a Masters in International Affairs from Columbia University.

She lives in New York with her husband and five children.